SMOKING
CIGARETTES
The Unfiltered Truth

Second Edition

SMOKING
CIGARETTES
The Unfiltered Truth

Understanding Why and How To Quit

Second Edition

Janet Benner, Ph.D.

Joelle Publishing, Santa Barbara, California

Smoking Cigarettes: The Unfiltered Truth
Understanding Why and How To Quit
Second Edition

Published by
>Joelle Publishing
>P. O. Box 91229
>Santa Barbara, CA 93190-1229
>*www.joellepublishing.com*

Design by Robert Howard Graphic Design
Printed in the United States of America
by Central Plains Book Manufacturing

Library of Congress Control Number 2002107024
ISBN 0-942723-16-3

To

Cynthia, Chris, Joey, and all of the staff
and members of the Tri-County Regional Team
who for nine years fought the good fight
to save our children from the tobacco industry.

Contents

Preface

For several years I have worked with people in their struggles with addictive behaviors: drugs, alcohol, overeating, you name it. Because of my own ordeal with cigarettes as well as my experience with others, I have come to believe that smoking is the single most dangerous habit, as well as the most difficult to overcome. With so many dying and becoming disabled because of tobacco, I decided to direct my efforts toward helping people in their choice to become nonsmokers.

It is a difficult and trying choice. Time and again I've watched intelligent people agonize over their relationships with cigarettes. It is a trap, pure and simple. A trap set intentionally by the tobacco industry. Nonetheless, most smokers berate themselves day after day for continuing to smoke even though they are convinced they are unable to stop.

If I accomplish nothing else with this book, I want to help people realize there is nothing stupid or weak about smoking, that the only way out is to forgive themselves and use their energies to seek solution.

Smokers are driven to maintain this behavior they often despise.

"But I enjoy it!" some might argue. "I don't want to quit."

When pinned down, smokers will admit they enjoy only 4 or 5 of the 10 to 80 cigarettes they smoke each day. The rest are smoked to maintain their habits. This is not a conscious choice. They maintain the habit because of a complex set of dynamics often beyond their control and certainly beyond their immediate awareness. It is truly a cruel paradox. The fact is, each time they inhale, smokers are severely undermining the quality of their daily lives and accelerating themselves toward early deaths.

The dynamics of the smoking habit are indeed complex, but the dangers of smoking are so real that it is crucial that each smoker be given the right information and appropriate assistance to make the important personal life choice to be a nonsmoker. I offer this book to that end. So, this book is for smokers and those who have loved ones who smoke. It is also a book for those who seek solution.

To begin your search for solution, be positive, have hope, and view each adventure with quitting as one step closer to accomplishing permanent and comfortable nonsmoking. It is possible for everyone. People no longer need to be slaves to this dangerous, debilitating, and hugely expensive liaison.

If you read this book from cover to cover you will have a better understanding of your addiction to tobacco, including smokeless, and a good chance at putting a stop to it. It will take hard work, dedication, desire, and certainly some anguish and discomfort. Preview the Strategies and Interventions in Chapter 3 now, if you choose. Really decide to do it, and it can happen for you.

Look forward to renewed health, energy, vitality, zest — once and forever, an end to the dangerous enslavement to the cigarette. For a price, its all yours. The price is an unbending resolve to make this dramatic and wonderful shift in your life. Do it now; there is no better time to quit. Understand that you are important; therefore, your health is important. Do it because you deserve it. Give yourself and your loved ones this wonderful gift, the best you could possibly give.

One of the questions put to me repeatedly in my classes is, "Who says so?" Stated differently, "How do you know this is true?" There are literally stacks and stacks of materials and literature and research about this business of smoking and tobacco addiction. While I attempt to simplify the ideas, it is a very complex issue. Instead of using unfriendly footnotes for every idea, I have chosen to cite sources in the text and include a bibliography in the back of the book.

At the time of this writing, there is still much being learned about how the brain is altered with addiction, and if the addictive substance is no longer ingested, how long it takes for the alterations to be corrected, for the brain to return to "normal." Someday we will have these answers, but for now, we don't. In my view, knowing all this may not be important to your quitting process, as long as we understand how to help you quit comfortably so that you may remain quit. Relapse is the most daunting question of all.

Also, in the chapter on resources, I have included a number of Web site addresses where you can do research of your own. It is a fascinating subject, and the more you know, the better handle you will have on your own smoking habit. You can answer your questions for yourself.

And a word about gender. Being a woman, I am aware of the practice of using the pronoun he to denote *he* or *she*.

Please excuse my following that convention. Currently, the pronoun *they* is also used to denote he or she. I can't bring myself to use the plural pronoun in a singular pronoun context. I don't know how to solve these problems without detracting from the real message here which is, female or male, it is time to stop smoking. Thank you for your indulgence.

Acknowledgments

For this, the second edition, the staff of the Santa Barbara County Department of Public Health, Dawn Dunn, Jan Koegler, and Petra Beumer, assisted with ideas, information, and editing as did Norman Russell and Harriet McNamara. Marilyn Scott was my master editor. Thanks for helping make this a readable and useful book.

My smokeless tobacco guru, Liz Cofer, gave invaluable assistance with Chapter 6, supplying information that is new to this edition. The ground-breaking work of Linda Ferry, M.D., in treating nicotine addiction provided insights into the use of pharmacotherapies. Dr. Andrew Weil continues to inform about a broad range of preventative healthcare considerations.

I would also like to acknowledge the California Department of Health Services Tobacco Control Section for its pioneer health education program that brought the smoking prevalence rate to 18% in California. I was part of that program for 12 years.

I freely used information from the U.S. Department of Health and Human Services and its Centers for Disease Control and Prevention as well as several Reports from the Surgeon General of the United States.

Thousands of courageous smokers and former smokers were the inspiration for the book; you can read some of their stories in Chapter 9.

The layout and cover were designed by Robert Howard Graphic Design.

Thanks to all, and to the many people who assisted me with support and information for the first edition.

Thanks to Norman, my family, friends, and colleagues for their unflagging support, patience, and love.

"I have the power to produce perfect
results in every area of my life."

*Love Lines: Affirmations for
the Mind/Body/Spirit*
By Joyce Strum

"I *am* responsible for what I see.
I choose the feelings I experience,
and I decide upon the goal I will achieve.
And everything that seems to happen to me
I asked for, and receive as I have asked."

A COURSE IN MIRACLES

Chapter

— 1 —

Why Should I Quit?

"I feel so strongly about the health risks of tobacco that I am unwilling to accept patients who are users unless they commit to attempting to quit."

Andrew Weil, M. D.

On November 29, 2001, George Harrison, the quiet, thoughtful Beatle, succumbed to a brain tumor at the age of 58. The news said only that he had died of cancer. In 1997 Harrison was treated for throat cancer, which he attributed to his many years of smoking. He was confident of his recovery, however, because he had given up smoking. But not soon enough. In 1999 he was treated for lung cancer, and ultimately, the cancer spread to his brain and killed him.

What a sad story. One of the icons of our time, his life cut short because of his deadly addiction. But there are many, many similar stories. All sad, all hideous. About 435,000 such stories unfold annually in the United States alone. Worldwide, the smoking epidemic rages; millions of people are doomed to untimely deaths. You do not have to be one of them.

Why Quit?

The reasons are endless. You have your own. Yet smokers have much in common. They desperately want to quit, go through the discomfort of quitting, and then find themselves smoking all over again. They ask themselves, "Why bother? The cure is worse than the disease. Why should I quit?"

Keep reading. Maybe you think you've heard it all. But just maybe, you'll discover something new here. Something that will give you a little push of motivation to keep you in the struggle.

At least understand this: *The more times you begin the quitting process, the more energy you put toward the goal of being a nonsmoker, the more likely you are to eventually achieve that goal.* It took me all of four years to finally become a permanent nonsmoker. Maybe you'll get lucky and it will only take you two years, or one, a month, a week?

In case anyone believes that clove cigarettes are basically more safe, you should know that methyleugenol, one of the main flavor components in the cigarettes, is listed as a carcinogen on the list by the CA Safe Drinking Water and Toxic Enforcement Act of 1986. And if you think switching to smokeless tobacco is a good alternative, read Chapter 6.

When deciding to give up cigarettes (tobacco), think about the quality of your everyday life. Smokers are living with two to four times as much carbon monoxide in their blood as nonsmokers. This, in itself, seriously impairs vitality and energy. It's sort of equivalent to taking a dose of strychnine everyday. A slow poison, a slow death. Like in an Alfred Hitchcock movie.

Nicotine is also a strong and deadly poison. *One drop of pure nicotine on your tongue would kill you in minutes.* It is sometimes used to put horses down when they break a leg.

Instead of using a gun, the poor animals are simply injected with nicotine.

When nicotine enters the system, something akin to the flight-or-fight reflex goes into play. The blood vessels, especially to the extremities, constrict. The heart rate increases by 10 to 20 beats. Blood pressure rises by 10 to 20 degrees. Fatty acids are released into the blood stream. Adrenaline is released and blood sugar rises. Of course, the smoker cannot flee or fight the invader, but the body works very hard to burn out and burn off the poison. This process alone robs the body of energy that would be used for more productive functions and keeps the smoker in varying states of intense activity and low, flat energy loss.

People think that smoking relaxes them. In fact, nicotine is a strong stimulant, and for the most part, people become noticeably calmer as they give up their cigarettes. It is an especially vicious cycle for people who might be described as hyperactive, very nervous, energetic people. They take cigarettes to keep themselves calm. They smoke more and more cigarettes depending on the stress in their lives. The result is that the cigarettes make them more hyper. They say they can't quit because smoking calms them down. Actually, the initial intake of nicotine does bring with it a chemical reaction that gives the smoker a momentary sense of relaxation and well-being. However, the overall result is the burning of energy at a heightened rate so that these smokers often feel fatigue coupled with hyper or agitated feelings. They are amazed at how much they slow down after they have been nonsmokers for only two or three days.

Smokers are constantly stimulated, so some do not sleep well. Many wake up in the night to smoke. Because of the high levels of stimulant in their systems, they do not experience the deep sleep of nonsmokers. Some smokers report that when they quit, they jump and twitch themselves awake several times in the night. Their bodies are not used to the new, deeper sleep. The body reacts as if it were going into unconsciousness and reflexively jars itself awake. This disturbed sleeping pattern passes in two or three days, and the new nonsmoker finds he requires less sleep now because he is sleeping so well.

And hear this! *An estimated 5.5 minutes of life are lost for each cigarette smoked.* The smoker has an average reduction in life expectancy of five to eight years. Since this is an average, and some smokers are living into their 80s, you may be risking many more than eight years of your life. If you add to your smoking a high-stress job and a few genetic factors, take 10 to 20 years off your life expectancy.

There is an old but highly effective film about smoking called "The Feminine Mistake", which shows a woman who is 43 and dying of lung cancer. She is shockingly, sadly thin and very confused about how this happened to her. She expected smoking to take maybe five years off the *other end* of her life.

"This is not that end," she says.

We are told she died six days after the segment was filmed.

The number of years you're trading also varies with the numbers of cigarettes smoked and the number of years you've been smoking. By the way, the younger you were when you started, the more risk there is to develop one of the diseases associated with smoking. This is especially true of emphysema. If, as a child, you suffered from asthma or had pneumonia or other lung disorders, your chances of disease as an adult increase even further. One young man in his early 20s had begun smoking regularly at the age of six. Yes, that's right, six. He was already very wheezy and hoarse.

You can put it all together for yourself and begin counting. What are you actually trading for the momentary gratification of smoking that cigarette? Pretty grim, don't you agree?

Smoking-Related Disease

The Centers for Disease Control and the Surgeon General Reports articulate it fairly well. In excess of 400,000 people die prematurely each year from preventable smoking-related disease. It is scandalous and outrageous. This means that more people die annually of preventable disease than in several wars combined —10 times as many as in auto accidents. Certainly more than die of AIDS and drug or alcohol addiction. In fact, one in every five deaths in the United States is smoking related.

Smoking is the leading contributor to heart disease, the number one killer in the United States, with 134,235 deaths. Include stroke, hypertension, and other cardiovascular diseases and the number is 179,820 deaths annually.

According to the largest-ever study on the effects of tobacco on atherosclerosis, both smoking and passive exposure to tobacco smoke can accelerate irreversible hardening of the arteries. The study, conducted at Wake Forest University, enrolled 10,914 people to examine all risk factors for the disease. The researchers found that smokers had a 50% increase in the rate of plaque accumulation in the carotid arteries, ex-smokers had a 25% increase, and those exposed to environmental tobacco smoke (ETS) a 20% increase.

Everyone knows about lung cancer. But did you also know that 116,920 people die of smoking-related lung cancer every year? Add other cancers like lung cancer from ETS, 3,000 annually, and such cancers as throat and bladder, and the number of deaths attributable to cancer is 151,322.

Respiratory diseases, such as pneumonia and bronchitis, add up to 84,475 deaths annually. Also included in this number is emphysema. The common name for one or more of these diseases combined is Chronic Obstructive Pulmonary Disease (COPD).

Emphysema is one of the most painful and crippling diseases associated with smoking. Breathing becomes progressively difficult as the lungs' air sacks become scarred and cease functioning. People who have emphysema have a ghastly gray pallor and can hardly walk across the room without stopping to rest. Their huffing and puffing is so sad, especially when we know the next step is an oxygen bottle strapped to their backs with tubes taped to their noses. Most eventually die of heart failure because of the strain all this has placed on their hearts. Many still attempt to smoke until their last days, even though they are fully aware that quitting smoking is the only way to arrest their disease.

If the victim of emphysema is able to quit, his breathing improves within 24 hours. Cigarette smoke constricts the bronchi and with the removal of cigarettes the bronchi open. Even the person who has advanced emphysema will notice improvement. (Read stories about emphysema patients in Chapter 9.) The lungs will not heal; once the damage is done there is no way to repair them. Nonetheless, as the gunk from cigarettes clears out, the undamaged parts of the lung can take over some of the breathing function the disease has curtailed. Also, the air he is now inhaling is more pure, allowing more oxygen to get to the lungs. Unfortunately, many victims of emphysema continue to smoke, caught in a terrible, deadly trap.

And these are not the only diseases linked to smoking. Smokers have many more colds and suffer far more often with chronic bronchitis, pneumonia, and asthma as described above. These conditions show marked improvement as soon as smoking is stopped.

The following cancers have a positive link with cigarette smoking: cancer of the larynx, other kinds of throat cancers, oral cancers, carcinoma of the esophagus, and cancer of the bladder. Cancer of the pancreas has increased as the numbers of smokers have increased. Studies indicate a relationship between smoking and cancer of the kidney. One study indicated that current or former smokers were nearly nine times likelier than nonsmokers to have breast cancer at an early age. Preliminary findings suggest that women who use smokeless tobacco face an eight-fold risk of developing breast cancer. It's clear that tobacco in any form is a significant cancer threat.

Certain types of ulcers are caused or exacerbated by tobacco constituents. Other stomach disorders, such as esophageal reflux disease, are linked to smoking and smokeless tobacco use, too.

There are, as you can see, multiple specific diseases directly connected with smoking. In each there is a relationship between the disease and the length of time the smoker has smoked and the numbers of cigarettes the smoker uses. In other words, the more and longer you smoke, the more likely you are to get one of these diseases.

Blood and Circulatory System

Generally speaking, any disease process will be made worse by smoking and better by not smoking. There are two reasons for this. One is that the blood acts as a delivery system for the body. It brings nutrients in and takes toxins and waste out. When the blood molecules are loaded with carbon monoxide, as they are in smokers, this delivery service is severely curtailed.

The second issue is the impaired circulatory system. Photos show that capillaries and blood vessels at the extremities are all but closed down as the cigarette is smoked and for several minutes after. Again, this impairment does not allow the blood to do its natural thing, does not allow it to get to the source of the illness to carry away waste and bring in nutrients.

Striking a note in the direction of vanity, the constriction of the capillaries and blood vessels is probably the culprit in the increased wrinkling of facial skin that occurs in smokers. Generally, a chronic, long-time smoker looks about 10 years older than a nonsmoker.

Some people report an improvement in eyesight when they give up cigarettes. This also relates to the constriction of the blood vessels when smoking. An ophthalmologist told me that while for most people there would not be a noticeable change in vision, the general health of the eyes will improve for everyone. Some notice the improvement with better vision. I love it, don't you?

Doctors tell people facing major surgery they must quit smoking. There is a particular hazard related to general anesthesia and smoking. The blood is loaded with carbon monoxide so more chemicals are needed to put the patient under. The patient is therefore harder to bring around after the surgery. Another problem is the excessive coughing which is typical of smokers. After surgery this coughing can cause terrible pain and endanger the incision. Because of the poor condition of the smoker's lungs, pneumonia is an added postoperative concern.

The decreased function of the circulatory system adds to all health concerns, but there are some diseases that are specific to this problem. One is known as Buerger's disease or Peripheral Vascular Disease. Seen more often in men, this disease can cause severe discomfort and the eventual loss of a foot or leg to gangrene. The only way to arrest the course of this disease is complete cessation of the use of tobacco. Although it is not a common disease, it is ugly and unhappy indeed.

One woman told me she was falling asleep at inappropriate times and too early in the evening. She had smoked two or three packs of cigarettes each day for about 45 years. Her doctor explained she was suffering brain damage because of lack of oxygen. She was told she must stop smoking to allow the carbon monoxide to clear so her brain could receive the oxygen needed for proper functioning.

A 45-year-old man complained of severe headaches caused by clogged arteries, a direct result of years of smoking. This hardening of the arteries, a primary cause of stroke and heart attack, can be caused by use of tobacco. It is known that a connection exists between smoking and high blood cholesterol, a prime suspect in arteriosclerosis.

While it is true that many people smoke without these symptoms and outcomes, if you add the right heredity to your smoking, the chances of having these health problems increase. For example, if your father died prematurely of heart disease, you'd better consider giving up smoking because your chances of following in your father's footsteps are greatly enhanced by smoking.

Smoking and Eyesight

The Journal of American Medical Association (JAMA) reports that people who smoke are two times more at risk for macular degeneration, a usually untreatable affliction that impairs the vision of an estimated 1.7 million Americans. Generally, the disease is found among the elderly, and years after the smoker has quit, the risk remains.

I have said earlier that many people tell me their eyesight improves when they quit cigarettes. At least one part of the reason is that the capillaries in the eye close down with the inhalation of cigarette smoke, reducing blood and oxygen to the eye. This is a simplistic explanation to a complex problem. Suffice it to say, eye diseases, including cataracts, are yet another aspect of the dangers of smoking. Apparently this risk diminishes over time.

Smoking and Pregnancy

Now let me sound this alarm the loudest. PREGNANT WOMEN MAY NOT SMOKE. It's that simple. Smoking during pregnancy has the potential for bringing the most unhappy consequence related to cigarette use because it involves the well-being of another, very innocent, human.

Nicotine and other chemicals ingested by the mother get into the fetus's bloodstream. This causes retardation in the baby's growth rate, and the baby will weigh as much as a pound less at birth than would be expected.

Babies of smoking mothers are 10% to 14% more likely to be born prematurely and are much more likely to have lung disorders. The unborn baby practices breathing by exercising his breathing mechanisms. Obviously there is no exchange of air involved. The baby is preparing his muscles to enable him to breathe after birth. As the mother inhales her cigarette, the breathing practice ceases for approximately an hour after the mama puts out her cigarette. We have films that show this.

The baby of a smoking mother is several times more likely to have cancer or heart disease after he is born. It's one thing to give yourself lung disease or cancer but to give it to your unborn child is quite another.

And after the baby is born? If you nurse? Mother continues to give her baby nicotine through her breast milk, continuing to lower baby's general immune system. This is serious, very serious. As I said before. PREGNANT WOMEN (AND NURSING MOTHERS) MAY NOT SMOKE.

And there is more about smoking around your babies and children.

Environmental Tobacco Smoke (ETS) and Children

The 1986 report, *The Health Consequences of Involuntary Smoking*, from the Surgeon General, reviewed the literature and presented copious scientific evidence addressing the relationship between parental smoking and respiratory illness among children. Hospital admissions for bronchitis and pneumonia are 28% greater for children whose parents smoke, and there is significantly more asthma among children of smokers.

An article in the *Journal of Pediatrics* in 2002 proves the connection between Sudden Infant Death Syndrome (SIDS) and smoking mothers. There are two factors in SIDS. The first is the position the baby is in while he sleeps (he should be on his back or side, not on his stomach) and the second is cigarette smoke. Lung tissue from babies who had died was tested for nicotine. SIDS babies had much more nicotine in their lungs. "What was found there must have happened soon before death. Nicotine has a short half life," the researcher said.

ETS and Others

The 1986 Surgeon General's report also states unequivocally that nonsmoking women married to smokers have an increased risk of heart disease. There is evidence that demonstrates the same connection for the nonsmoking wife with emphysema and other lung diseases.

And think about those beloved pets who live in a home with a smoker. They are being exposed to ETS and are also suffering the consequences. One quitter told me that the vet had told her that her doggie had lung disease. That was a primary reason for her quitting.

In Chapter 8 the ETS issue is discussed further.

Chapter One

Smoking and Impotence

The CDC reported in 1994 that men who smoke are 50% more likely to suffer from impotence than are non-smokers. The rate may even be higher because some men are unwilling to acknowledge the sexual disorder. The study, published in the *American Journal of Epidemiology*, was the first to show that smoking alone is a risk factor for impotence. The cause of this problem is not known but is probably associated with vascular disease. Other possible culprits are the different components in cigarette smoke, such as carbon monoxide, which can relax the blood vessels or affect the nervous system.

In 1999, on the TV show, "60 Minutes", the President of the American Medical Association, Dr. Randolf Smoak, along with other doctors, presented an in-depth report on the problem. The doctors warned that the impotence rate among smokers is nearly double the rate for nonsmokers and further cautioned that teens smoking two packs each day will likely begin to have impotence problems before the age of 30.

In another study, a team from the New England Research Institutes followed 513 men for 10 years and found moderate or complete impotence in 26% of the nonsmokers exposed to ETS both at home and at work. The rate of impotence for men reporting no exposure was 14%.

The California Department of Health Services Tobacco Control Section ran an amusing TV ad that reflected the link between impotence and smoking. The ad really opened some eyes.

Smoking and Women

As the number of women smokers increased, so did the incidence of lung cancer in women. This disease has now surpassed breast cancer as the number one cancer killer of women (35,741 deaths annually). The concerns for women smokers do not stop there. Because of the female's complex hormonal makeup, she risks more than the male smoker. For example, women should not take birth control pills if they smoke because the incidence of clotting is increased. One woman quit smoking because her doctor refused to prescribe the female hormones an early hysterectomy made necessary. The doctor was afraid the troublesome clots she once had in her legs would recur. There is a very sad story about Marlene, another clotting victim, in Chapter 9.

There is strong evidence that nicotine interferes with the assimilation of calcium in the body, thus smokers, especially women, are much more prone to developing osteoporosis. So it is clear that women are risking even more than men when continuing their smoking habits year after year.

Other Related Issues

Besides osteoporosis, there are other serious musculoskeletal problems. Some of these are disc degeneration, slow healing of fractures and incisions from surgery, and spinal compression fractures. Back pain from work-related injury is more common in smokers. About 50% of workers who smoke complain of lower back pain compared to 20% of nonsmokers, says Dr. Edward N. Hanley, Chairman of the Orthopedic Surgery Department at the Carolinas Medical Center in Charlotte, N.C.

Do you wish to lose your teeth to periodontal disease? Wear false teeth, then. Or quit smoking. Your teeth are probably yellow from tobacco stains anyway.

Certainly the risk to health and vitality is the most compelling reason why one would choose to give up smoking. But there are many other reasons why people make the decision to quit.

When we consider the hazards of smoking, we sometimes forget one of the biggest. Fire. One quarter of all fires involving mortalities are caused by cigarettes: improper disposal, smoking in bed, accidentally dropped cigarettes, ashes smoldering in furniture. We are talking about 1,500 deaths annually and 4,000 serious injuries. Many of the victims are innocent children. The cost of fires caused by cigarettes is in the millions of dollars each year. Couldn't we find better ways of using this money?

In many parts of the country it is socially unacceptable to smoke. We are becoming a country of closet smokers. Smokers can no longer smoke in airplanes, and if smoking is allowed at all in restaurants, it is in obscure sections. Nonsmoking zealots (like me) are more vocal about being in smoke-filled rooms. One unfortunate lady in her 60s went to visit her daughter and found no smoking signs in the car, on the porch, everywhere inside the house. The woman was so offended she vowed never to return to her daughter's home.

Increasingly, smoking is illegal in public places. Ordinances of all kinds are springing up, making it more uncomfortable to smoke.

Many businesses are dealing with the smoking and ETS problems by introducing policies that do not allow smoking on the premises or allow smoking only in designated areas. Fortunately some companies are assisting their employees with on-site smoking-cessation programs. Many companies no longer hire workers who smoke. (Smoking in workplaces is against the law in California and several other states.)

Other Important Reasons Why People Quit

For thousands of people, the habit interferes with important choices. Often a smoker will choose to pass up an otherwise suitable job because of the smoking policies of the employer.

People still make life decisions that are directed at maintaining a behavior that is killing them. Seems like madness, doesn't it? But read Chapter 2 about what keeps people smoking, and you will understand that they are enslaved to buying, carrying, bumming, and lighting and inhaling cigarettes. They are slaves to the emptying of ashtrays and running about cleaning up dropped ashes and other messes. *The ugly fact of not being in control of their lives, of being slaves to the disgusting things, is one of the main reasons people choose to make an effort to quit.*

And cigarettes are disgusting. They are filthy and smelly. And a terrible nuisance! Smokers will not leave the house without being fully equipped. People stop in the middle of whatever they may be doing if they feel an urge. These can be important meetings or recreational activities. No matter what, if they get an urge, they are compelled to respond. Woe is me, what a bother.

Many people have consulted me on what to do about their loved ones who smoke. (See Chapter 7.) Conflict over smoking can wreck an otherwise viable alliance. Some describe kissing a smoker as being like kissing an ashtray. Not too nice. And the smoker feels as bad about it as the nonsmoker though he may appear to be angered by the fuss.

And the cost! If you smoke one pack, 20 cigarettes each day, you will spend close to $150 a month or $1,800 a year. That could pay the gas and water bill for most families. If you smoke for 30 years you will spend more than $54,000, or for two packs each day, around $108,000! So it's an expensive habit; yet another reason why people choose to quit.

Chapter One

Lifestyle is another big consideration in quitting. Many people quit smoking because of involvement with their churches or religious groups. Others quit because of physical activities, like body building or running. These activities are severely curtailed by smoking, and smoking becomes more and more a roadblock to reaching physical goals. Others want to quit because they are in medically related professions. Doctors and nurses smoke, too, and for the same reasons anyone else does.

So the reasons for quitting are multiple: cancer, heart disease, lung disorders like chronic obstructive pulmonary disease (COPD), all manner of other related health considerations, fire, cost, enslavement to the cigarette, social and employment issues, relationship problems, lifestyle. And the list goes on. Reason after reason why people decide it's time. It's time to quit. And now you know, it's time to quit for you, too.

Chapter
— 2 —

Why Can't We Just Quit?

"I have an intolerable burning, tingling all over my body. I cannot bear quitting."

Hypoglycemic man

Sneaking out to the garage for a quick puff, standing in the rain to smoke because smoking is no longer allowed in your building, brushing your teeth several times each day so no one will know you really haven't quit, and on and on. As smokers, we do all this stuff to make it possible to keep our habits going. Self-loathing and self-deprecation are part of the picture, lying in bed at night berating ourselves for continuing to do these amazingly ridiculous rituals. And the expense. At the time of this writing, the cost of one pack of cigarettes approaches $5.00. Either we are in deep denial, or we are hating ourselves for continuing year after year to do homage to our enslavement to tobacco.

Why can't we just quit? Of 100 smokers, 95 or so will say that if they could just quit without all the pain and heartache they have experienced in the past with quitting, they surely would. Most smokers would give up their cigarettes if there were a magic bullet. Since there is none, health educators like me continue to look for ways to make the process feel like that magic bullet.

The quitting process can be facilitated to a degree by information concerning the "why" of the smoking addiction/habit. The dynamics of the habit are complex but not incomprehensible.

To begin with, there is research evidence that the propensity to become a smoker is inborn. It is clear that if a parent or parents smoke, the children are 75% more likely to smoke than kids who come from nonsmoking families. The nature-versus-nurture discussion is probably not very helpful because the end results and solutions are the same. Nonetheless, some people are more susceptible to becoming hooked on cigarettes than others. Don't we all know the guy who just smokes at parties? Or the woman who carries the same pack with her for two weeks, having one or two each day? It's hard not to be envious of such people, isn't it?

Nonetheless, with laboratory animals there seems to be a difference in the way the brain receptors respond to nicotine. This difference would have been genetically programmed before birth. The problem is that a person has to get a good habit going before he realizes he is susceptible to getting a good habit going. However, once the smoker breaks his habit, he can look on it the same way he views an allergy to strawberries.

"Strawberries give me a rash, so I don't eat them."

"Smoking cigarettes hooks me and I keep wanting more, so I don't use them."

Few smokers who have had a hefty habit will ever be able to smoke socially; that is, smoke *just one* without wanting another.

The smoker who quits must have a clear understanding and acceptance of his susceptibility, or he will find himself restimulating his habit over and over again. *The recidivism or relapse rate for smoking is from 85% to 90%.* Some studies say it's higher. In other words, if 100 people in the United States quit today, only 10 to 15 of those will be permanent nonsmokers. Dismal statistics, right? Let's set about to change these numbers. You too can join the troops of the successful.

The Physical Addiction

People don't talk so much anymore about "nicotine fits." What is one, anyway? A nicotine fit is a strong urge to smoke. As you probably know, it is the nicotine in the cigarette that is physically addictive. This after the new smoker has worked his way through choking coughs and feelings of nausea and dizziness encountered when first practicing smoking. (One quitter said cigarettes continued to make him sick long after he was a regular smoker. He just didn't smoke early in the day or he would throw up.) With continued smoking, the nicotine begins to alter the chemical motivational reward system of the body. For some people, it takes only a matter of days of continued smoking for neurological changes to take place.

The repeated ingestion of nicotine interferes with production of one or more neurotransmitters, part of our chemical reward system. There is still much discussion about what really happens in the brain, how the brain changes. For example, some researchers say that with the ingestion of an addictive substance, there is a dopamine spike, which means a pleasure spike. Others say they are unable to establish a clear dopamine connection with nicotine. Some say neurological recovery occurs within a few days, some say within six months, and some say the brain never fully recovers.

What we know for sure is, when the nicotine isn't present for a few hours, its absence, along with the absence of the natural chemical function, causes the feeling of uneasiness or even panic we know as an urge to smoke. Withdrawal is occurring. We then take the cigarette to make our bodies feel right, that is, to rebalance our physiological systems. *We take a cigarette to fix what it, in fact, has caused.* Thus the loop of the physical addiction. It has been said that nicotine is comparable to heroin and cocaine in its addictive properties. The physical addiction to nicotine is very complex, and as I said, some researchers believe that the brain is altered, if not permanently, at least for a long time.

Endorphins are released in the brain seven seconds after inhalation. Endorphins are our natural tranquilizer/ painkillers, and in the past, some researchers have said this is the primary component in addiction and withdrawal symptoms. Clinicians even devised a clip that the tobacco quitter clipped to his nose causing mild pain that released endorphins. We believe that exercise is no doubt a more comfortable method of replacing that good feeling of endorphin release when you quit smoking.

Within three to four days from the time the smoker quits smoking, the nicotine is completely washed from his system. Though there is still some question, we think the chemical reward system is soon restored. Quitters report good feelings they have not felt in years. The problem is, even after three or four days of not smoking, some former smokers continue to have urges that drive them to distraction. They are still obsessed with wanting a cigarette. The "nicotine fits" continue. So what else is going on?

Learning/Conditioning

One of the strangest and most intriguing things about what it is to be human is that we can know for a certainty that an activity is bad for us and yet return time and time again to that activity. We are creatures of habit, so returning to certain behaviors becomes habitual. Mostly these behaviors carry with them an initial, if not lasting, pleasure. The pleasure is sensory, and the activity registers in our unconscious memory as being pleasurable. Because it is pleasurable, our unconscious tells us it is "good" for us. We condition ourselves to do things much as we train our animals, through a system of rewards. The pleasure is the reward, and the activity will probably continue as long as it continues to give pleasure.

The *conditioned response*, the learning, is an essential part of the cigarette-smoking habit. When the cigarette is lit, the smoker takes a deep and relaxing inhalation. Shortly thereafter the nicotine in the system causes the release of adrenaline and a rise in blood sugar, these events serving to give the smoker a mild lift. And as I said, within seven seconds, endorphins are released from the brain giving the smoker a temporary sense of well-being. Some say there is a dopamine spike. These pleasant sensations, coupled with taking the cigarette to stop the physical withdrawal symptoms, register in the unconscious over and over—*teaching* the smoker that smoking is *good* and rewarding the smoker for smoking.

If we say that the smoking habit is a learned behavior, that it resides in the unconscious, away from intellectual access, then we can more clearly understand the involuntary nature of the habit and why people continue to smoke. Smokers, therefore, have learned unconsciously that smoking is good while knowing intellectually that it is killing them.

A majority of smokers, 80% to 90%, began to smoke when they were in their early teens. Teenagers view the dangers of the diseases related to smoking as being light-years away. Teenagers and young adults also have a sense of being indestructible. By the time some maturation sets in, they have registered thousands of pleasant associations with cigarettes in their unconscious memory systems. Now they begin to think perhaps smoking is not such a great thing to do. They wake up each morning with a cough and notice a slight shortness of breath when they are out jogging or playing tennis. Unfortunately, by now they are well hooked and have become successful smokers. All this without really assessing or understanding how they became so expert at this unfortunate behavior.

The expertise that the person has acquired through his smoking career is exemplified by the fact that when the time comes that he decides it is time to quit, and it comes for every smoker, he cannot simply put aside his pack of cigarettes. Many smokers have learned so thoroughly in their unconscious memory that smoking is good for them that they are prodded and tricked by their own unconscious into continuing their habits.

Quitting smoking is one of the most difficult things a person will ever do because of the conditioning that has taken place unbeknownst to him. The urges and anxiety come, in part, from a deep belief that he is not aware of that cigarettes *help him survive*. The conflict between this unconscious belief and his conscious decision to quit causes such discomfort that he will often go back to smoking to end the agony.

Psychological/Social Issues

The physiological addiction and unconscious conditioning just described are always a part of the smoking habit. But there are other aspects of smoking that are unique to different individuals. These complicate the stopping process but still do not make it impossible. Understanding these will facilitate success.

One such consideration might be termed "emotional." Some people are as attached to their cigarettes as they might be to a friend or lover. They seem to project onto the cigarette attributes that have nothing whatever to do with the physical properties or capabilities of the cigarette. These smokers believe that cigarettes enable them to cope, that life without cigarettes would be drab and uninteresting. Cigarettes become the single most important thing in their lives. Without them, these folks could not function day to day, or so they believe. This thinking reinforces the learned behavior and makes things doubly difficult.

Often the people who have the imagination to form this sort of attachment also have the intelligence to know how damaging cigarettes are to their health. They, therefore, face constant conflict and considerable discomfort. To many, smoking is contrary to their lifestyles and their health philosophies, but the attachment is so strong that quitting is terribly painful and frightening. Many in the health care professions have this experience: nurses, doctors, dieticians and medical technicians. People who are concerned with physical fitness and work out regularly are also among the types of people who are in serious conflict over their smoking addictions.

Women often express concern about possible weight gain when they quit. They have an acculturated belief that they will no longer be lovable or likable with extra weight; therefore, they must continue to smoke, or once quit, they must start again even though one-third of the adult population of the U.S. is overweight. Someone must like some of these people. To begin to approach the harm being done to their health by cigarettes, they would have to gain 50 pounds or more.

Many smokers describe a kind of internal battle they have with themselves. It takes the form of, "You can't tell me what to do!" I refer to it as the bad-boy syndrome. We seem to be a stubborn species, even if what we take a stand for is likely to damage our health. I've noticed this type of thinking on several occasions with very ill people. They know they have to quit but something tells them not to be pushed into it. Perhaps this relates to what we know as free will. Their stubbornness is not directed at me, nor at their doctors, nor at their loved ones, but rather, it seems, at themselves.

But overall, stubbornness is not a bad thing. This same firmness of attitude can be channeled into working toward quitting.

Many smokers use cigarettes as a reward for small tasks completed.

"All right, as soon as I finish this letter, I get to have a cigarette."

This also implies a break in activity, a time-out. Since lots of people are attempting to smoke less, their reward system may stretch the time between cigarettes.

"Okay, I'll wait 'til three, then stop for a smoke."

This makes cigarettes all the more important and rewarding. Better to state it like it is:

"Okay, by three I'll have to have a cigarette or I'll go nuts," making the cigarette more the villain than the reward.

Other smokers use smoking as an organizational device. They get up in the morning and light a cigarette, take a shower, light a cigarette, put on makeup, light a cigarette, and decide what to wear with the help of a cigarette. If the cigarette is withdrawn, they feel helplessly disoriented (a condition that passes in a few short days when they quit.)

Less dramatically, for lots of people, smoking affords a certain identity. It is a kind of social lubricant. Offering, accepting, and lighting cigarettes provides something to do in social situations. It is portrayed in advertising as glamorous and/or manly so people feel, in some ways, more glamorous when smoking. Smoking in movies also adds to the illusion. While about 24% of the adult population smokes, in movies more than 70% of the characters smoke. Even though there are influences in our culture urging us to smoke, in some areas public smoking laws and changes in the way smoking is perceived have caused smoking to become more and more a social embarrassment.

As we said, the majority of people begin their smoking careers as teenagers and pre-teens. It is perceived by these young people to be one of the first steps toward liberation from their parents, family, and school authorities. For some, the need to separate, which is very natural, becomes a rebellious process. Smoking, to the dismay of parents, is part of that process. For lots of kids, smoking is primarily a recreational activity and is perceived as cool. Of course, if you asked a teenager why he smoked he would say either, "I don't know" or "I like it." Perhaps he would even say, "Everyone does." It's not cool to say they smoke because it's cool.

When relating psychological/social ties with cigarettes to why people begin to smoke, the most clear answer would be, a sense of identity. It gives the teenager a tie with his peer group, makes him feel more grown up, and adds to separation from his family.

Unfortunately most youth believe they could quit immediately if they chose to. Recent research shows that youth become addicted much more readily and rapidly than they believe. Within a few days of smoking a few cigarettes each day, the youthful smoker begins to show signs of being addicted.

The Habit

Consider that if you smoke one pack each day you will be bringing that cigarette to your mouth from 150 to 200 times, 10 or so times for each cigarette. Double that for two packs. Smokers probably do this single activity more than any other in their lives.

After years of smoking, some of the activities surrounding smoking become almost reflexive. Men talk about reaching to their breast pockets and patting for a cigarette years after they have quit smoking. Women tell of getting up from their chairs, going across the room to their purses, and searching for something — cigarettes, of course. While driving, people feel around on the car seat for their cigarettes or on the couch next to them while watching TV. And they no longer smoke.

Many people report having no consciousness of reaching for, lighting, and setting in the ashtray cigarettes they suddenly notice burning there. So the activities related to smoking seem to have a life of their own, and when the smoker quits, some of the feeling of loss comes from eliminating these activities. Smokers wonder aloud about what they will do with their hands. How will they ever get used to not having cigarettes to fiddle with? But they learn, and not too long after quitting, in about three weeks, the habits associated with smoking become distant memories for the majority of former smokers.

Hypoglycemia

A small percentage of smokers are hypoglycemic. In some circles the condition is more or less ignored, but since I believe it can pose a serious threat to quitting, I will include it here.

Hypoglycemia is a condition in which the regulatory mechanism for blood sugar is faulty. The blood sugar level frequently drops below normal, causing multiple symptoms, including shakiness and irritability, when the person is hungry. A candy bar can alleviate the symptoms by raising the blood sugar level, but a rebound effect is inevitable causing an even sharper drop. Food will correct the situation temporarily but unless a carefully planned nutritional regimen is followed, one that eliminates sugar, the unpleasant symptoms will occur again and again. Other symptoms include mood swings, frequent illness, sometimes fainting, disorientation, and more. There is an excellent book, by J. Saunders, titled *Hypoglycemia: The Disease Your Doctor Won't Treat*. It is probably now out of print, but if you suspect you might be hypoglycemic you may want to try to find it.

What does this have to do with smoking? Remember I said that when the cigarette was inhaled there was an increase in blood sugar? For hypoglycemic people this represents a real trap. Their blood sugar levels become regulated by the cigarette, and the conditioning process is enhanced. They become addicted to the blood sugar elevations as well as to the nicotine.

When hypoglycemics stop smoking they can really crash. The blood sugar level fluctuates dramatically, tossing them about on a sea of emotional upheaval and physical symptoms that are nightmarish. One gentleman told me he had an intolerable burning, tingling all over his body, and he could not bear quitting. Another man told me he was beside himself with discomfort, sitting in the shower stall, wanting to die, until he ate a couple of spoonfuls of sugar.

In general, because of their more complex physiology, women suffer from this sort of thing more frequently.

Belief System

Our beliefs are formed through sensory and intellectual experiences throughout our lives. These beliefs, our view of things, affect how we behave. In other words, our perceptions tend to accommodate our beliefs, as does our behavior. Perception and behavior create our reality. We do not behave in ways that are out of concert with what we believe. Thus, what we believe, essentially, creates our reality.

In my smoking-cessation classes, we discuss this little paradigm. People hold all kinds of beliefs related to their smoking habits. For example, if someone believes he will have a very difficult time quitting, he certainly may have a difficult time quitting. It would be helpful for you to check out your attitudes toward smoking. Do you believe it helps you hold down your weight, so it would be best not to quit? Do you believe the cigarette is your best friend and you will miss it for a long, long time? Do you have mixed beliefs about it, like you know it is damaging to your health but you believe you are powerless over it?

The idea is to check out what you believe, and if you see that your beliefs will not be helpful to your quitting process, change them by reframing them. For example, if you now believe that the cigarette is your best friend, reframe the idea to, "I have been thinking cigarettes are my best friend, but they are not because they are hurting me. My best friends do not do me harm."

Right now there are only two things you need to believe: it's time to quit and you can do it.

We have discussed several components that make up your smoking dependence: the physical addiction, the conditioned learning, the psychosocial aspect, the habit or the behavior itself, hypoglycemia, and your belief system. Some smokers lean more to one aspect of the problem than others. Some have a combination of all, and some have some whole other thing going on.

At least you now understand that continuing smoking does not imply the smoker is weak. And you should be clear that smoking does not mean the smoker is stupid. Smoking is a terrible trap. Some lucky people have an easier time extricating themselves from the trap than others do.

Now you have an understanding of why the quitting process can be so difficult and why you can be proud of yourself for confronting it head on. Hooray for you! The majority of people who quit do so without the help of professionals. They quit on their own. Such courage, such an undertaking. And you will do it, too.

Chapter
— 3 —

Strategies and Interventions

"I have made a commitment to myself
only to smoke in the shower.
With the water on, of course!"

Father Peter

G ood news! There are multiple solutions to your smoking habit. There are many groups who want to help you quit smoking and many smoking-cessation programs available to you. They range in cost from free or a few dollars to $700. The Internet offers a variety of materials and information of interest to you as you begin your quitting process. You will find a list of resources and how to use them in Chapter 10.

It is well known that most smokers who quit actually quit on their own. We will explore several strategies which will assist you in doing this, too. You can become the change agent in your own life and quit smoking for just the cost of this book. And why not?

All of the following strategies take energy and commitment. Set aside two weeks. Plan for this time to be very focused. It may be intense, but you will discover new things about yourself. So view your process as an adventure during which you will learn a lot as well as accomplish a goal that is very important to you and your family and friends. A goal that will add years to your life while making it richer and better.

Your first task is to set a *Quit Date;* then you can map out your plan. Read this chapter thoroughly. Choose exactly which strategies you intend to incorporate into your process and decide to stick to them.

Have a sense of humor about everything that happens in your quitting process. Be able to laugh at yourself. That way, you will be able to try some of the more absurd ideas. Smoking is basically absurd. It is an ironic joke played on us by our culture, the tobacco industry, its advertising, and, of course, ourselves. Remember the old Bob Newhart bit where he's talking on the telephone to Sir Walter Raleigh?

"What, Walt? You roll up these leaves. And what? Put 'em in your mouth...and you light 'em? Uh, Walt, isn't that a little dangerous?"

If you think about it, it's all pretty funny. Keep your sense of humor about smoking and about yourself. It will be easier.

A word of caution: DO NOT SUBSITTUTE FOOD FOR SMOKING. As you quit smoking, your metabolism will slow a bit and you may be a little more hungry. Nicotine suppresses appetite. The average weight gain with quitting is only three or four pounds, but be careful. If you eat to soothe a smoking urge, that, too, can become a problem with which you will have to deal. Watch yourself from the beginning, and weight gain need not be an issue.

AND DO NOT USE A PIPE OR SNUFF OR OTHER SPIT TOBACCO OR CIGARS AS SUBSTITUTES. All are equally addicting and can only cause you further grief. (See Chapter 6.) You may, of course, use the strategies given here to quit those things, too.

We hear people say, "I'm trying to quit smoking," as they go through the process of becoming a permanent non-smoker. They may not have smoked for several days, and they still say they are "trying to quit." In fact, they *have* quit! What they are trying to do now is get *comfortable* about it. You will notice that throughout this book I refer to quitting as choosing to become or becoming a nonsmoker. The word *trying* is self-defeating. There is inherent in it the possibility of failure, a back-door escape hatch. *Trying* means you may not be able. We prefer *doing*: I am doing the process of becoming a nonsmoker.

Remember, every time you venture into the world of quitting, you are closer to a permanent cure. Therefore, there are no failures. *Each start is part of an ongoing process*; thus, there is no trying, only doing. As soon as you decide to quit, you begin the process of doing the business of becoming a permanent nonsmoker. I refer to all related activities, therefore, as *the process*.

Okay, here we go to the *strategies*, also known as *interventions*.

Strategy #1: Negative/Positive Thoughts

I have become convinced, over the years of working with hundreds of cigarette quitters, that the process of becoming a nonsmoker is largely a mind game. You have read about all the physiological and learned things that keep you smoking, but the essential issue in quitting is keeping your attitude in the right place. Attitude and determination...no will power in our vernacular. Will power implies weakness if you're not immediately successful with quitting. Balderdash. Your smoking habit is much more complex than that.

Lead, polonium, aldehydes, cyanide, carbon monoxide, acetone, and of course, nicotine. Nice list, huh? These are some of the 4,000 chemicals, gases, and yuckahs you ingest when you smoke a cigarette.

From the time you make your decision to quit, begin to think about cigarettes in the worst possible light, something like this:

"Oh, yes, there's an urge. But cigarettes taste and smell awful. They are cyanide and acetone. I wouldn't give that stuff to my worst enemy. And they are a terrible bother. Before, I couldn't go out of the house without them. Now I am free of the nasty things."

Don't take the attitude that you are depriving yourself of something, feeling a little sorry for yourself. Recall, that something is killing you!

Do not allow yourself to reminisce about pleasant times associated with smoking. For example:

"I used to love to read and smoke."

Or,

"I love a good cigarette after a meal."

Of course, this is an oxymoron. There is no such thing as a "good" cigarette.

For some people there may be a time that resembles grieving. Do not deny these feelings but rather, reframe them, saying to yourself, "I see. I'm missing cigarettes, but they are nicotine and carbon monoxide. Poisonous."

Turn it around as quickly as you can without denying it.

"This is the new me. And I will be cleaner, healthier, and better. No question about it."

So keep all thoughts about cigarettes as negative as possible. Conversely, keep thoughts about the process you're going through as positive as possible.

"Hmmm, I'm feeling a bit disoriented today but who cares? That's all part of beating that damned habit. Hooray, I'm doing it!"

Acknowledge uncomfortable feelings:

"Hello, I'm feeling a bit fatigued."
Then reframe them.
"But, isn't this wonderful? This means it is happening. I'm doing it!"
And of course, you are!

Strategy #2: A Support System

If you do not already have one, develop a support system. By announcing to your friends and associates that you are in the process of becoming a nonsmoker, you are making a public commitment and might be a little embarrassed if you don't achieve immediate success (remember, every start brings you closer). To avoid feeling that kind of pressure, you may choose not to make this sort of announcement.

That is your choice. But you will need to tell a few people to establish your process support system, people you can call to talk it out with if you have an especially difficult moment.

It's nice to have a special smoking friend join you in the process. You can support each other with phone calls at any time of the day or night. You both will have read this book so will be able to go over strategies together.

"Joanie, I'm blowing it. Jake and I had a fight and I think I have to smoke."

"Huh uh, Janie. Now take a deep breath. (Pause.) You'll feel better in a minute. Did you play your tape? You know how that relaxes you. Or why not write in your journal? You know smoking now would only make you feel worse. It fixes absolutely nothing."

"I know, but it's so darned hard sometimes. I feel terrible. Maybe I should try the tape."

"Janie, you know that it is not giving up the cigarettes that's making you feel terrible. It's your fight with Jake. Try to separate the two things."

Chapter Three

"Yeah, Joanie, you're right. Maybe I'll take a bubble bath, then listen to the tape. I guess I'm already feeling better. Thanks, Joanie, you're a dear."

See how easy it can be with a buddy?

Do some things with people who don't smoke. You probably have a special friend or relative who has been concerned about your smoking. Plan to see him or her for lunch. Celebrate your new health and freedom with this special person. Enjoy sitting chatting in the restaurant without worrying about when you'll be able to have your next cigarette. If you live outside of California, enjoy sitting with your friend in the nonsmoking section. Be proud of yourself. Be happy.

Those friends of yours who are still smoking will require a slightly different approach. Tell them early on what you plan to do. Ask them for their support. Be careful to do it tactfully so they don't feel you are judging them. You know smokers tend to get defensive about their habits. When they see you quitting, it is a wakeup call that what they are doing to themselves is dangerous and they may have to do something about it. You can say something like,

"Greg, it's my time to become a nonsmoker. Can you help me by not smoking around me for a few days? We are such good smoking buddies, it's going to be hard at times. But with your help and support, I intend to do it."

Those people who care about you will be helpful, supportive, and happy for you. With their assistance and support, your process will be much easier for you.

Strategy #3: A Journal

Buy a stenographer's notebook to use as a journal. You can keep a diary of the events of your smoking cessation adventure (program). As people make the crucial decision to quit, then successfully put smoking behind them forever, they learn a lot about themselves. It's nice to record what happens. You can also use the journal as a kind of outlet. For example you might write,

"Right now the urge is tremendous so I choose to write about it instead of giving in to it. Let's see, what exactly am I feeling? My heart seems to be pounding a little. I feel disoriented, so it's somewhat difficult to write this. Actually, I feel a little afraid...Ah, but now it has subsided as if I couldn't keep feeling it and writing about it at the same time."

You get the idea. This is a good example of an intervention. You put a wedge between you and the feeling. You intervene.

You can log what you eat to make certain you aren't overeating. You can log the urges, as you might labor pains. Make a graph. You will notice the urges decreasing as you refuse to succumb to them. Some people feel anger at their predicament, irritated at finding themselves so hooked when getting themselves unhooked is so uncomfortable. Sometimes they're angry at being deprived of their cigarettes. If you notice yourself becoming angry, you can vent your anger on the pages of your journal. For example, you might direct your anger where it belongs:

"Damn Philip Morris, the whole lot, for making the damned things look so glamorous. Damn Janet Benner for writing this book and getting me into this uncomfortable position. Damn the cigarette. It is an evil little critter that has nearly wrecked my health, my life, and I thought it was my friend. Oh, damn, I feel so awful. But, of course, now I'm putting it all behind me. I am saving my life. I am doing the right and smart thing. (Thank you, Janet Benner, I take it back.)"

Even if you use your journal to vent, be sure to turn the anger around to a *positive thought*, to *positive energy*. Like it says above, "Now I am putting it all behind me, I am saving my life."

Chapter Three

Use your journal for poetry:

Smoking, smoking, puff, puff
Coughing, choking, enuff, enuff
Again I swear I'll quit today,
I'll save my life, hooray, hooray.

Or use the journal for recipes, for directions to a new city you're planning to visit. Use writing as an alternative behavior to smoking. Let your journal be your friend and confidant. It is for you, and no one else will read it unless you invite them to.

Have fun with it.

Strategy #4: Countdown/Cut Down

This consists of counting the numbers of cigarettes you smoke each day by going to a calendar or your journal and logging each cigarette you smoke. The trick is to be certain you smoke fewer each day, cutting down.

I invented such a method for myself and quit this way several times. It was effective for me because by the time I got down to two or three cigarettes a day, they became obnoxious tasting and made me dizzy and nauseous. My body was essentially detoxified by that time, and I no longer had tolerance for the nasty things. Then it was easier to quit altogether.

It also helped to begin the countdown with a brand of cigarettes other than my usual, one I really didn't like. Once I changed to Camel nonfilter, which nearly killed me, once I used Pall Mall in this way, and once I used something called lettuce cigarettes. Hmmm. All were even more repulsive than my regular brand.

Most of the literature on cessation says a "cold turkey" stop-all-at-once approach is more effective than my cut-down-gradually approach. The key here, again, is setting that quit day; otherwise you might be tapering for a long, long time.

Used properly, this strategy can be very helpful, especially if you don't plan to use Nicotine Replacement Therapy (NRT). (See Chapter 10.)

Strategy #5: Alternative Behaviors

Alternative behaviors are selected, directed actions that the new nonsmoker takes to make his process easier.

We are creatures of habit. We do the same things day after day in the same ways. For smokers, smoking is in some way associated with many daily activities. If you change one part of the activity, the association with smoking is interrupted so the "I need to smoke while I do this" pattern is minimized.

Make a list of your own smoking associations: before work with coffee, after lunch, on the telephone, in the car, after dinner, and so on. Be aware of the times and places and activities that you have always associated with smoking.

For example, you are accustomed to sitting in your special chair, watching T.V. each evening, your ashtray next to you along with all the other smoking paraphernalia. You must immediately remove and dispose of all the smoking-related items, but you may wish to replace them with something, perhaps a nice glass of ice water. You might also think about an alternative behavior. Perhaps knitting while you sit in your favorite chair and watch television. You men can do this, too. Or try some needlepoint, or get a pad and pencil and doodle on the paper. Or doodle in your journal. I have been giving yo-yos as prizes to my cigarette quitters. Yo-yos provide a fun intervention...something to do with your hands.

Or if this isn't enough to make you comfortable, re-arrange the furniture in the room, placing your special chair in a different location. This can be effective in your office, your bedroom, den, garage, wherever you were accustomed to smoking. The changed environment helps dispose of troublesome associations.

People use cigarettes for a "time-out". They tell co-workers they need a cigarette break, so they leave the office to go to the specific area where smoking is allowed. (In California, all places of business, including bars, are smoke-free to protect workers from second-hand smoke.) Learn to take a break or a time-out by simply saying, "I need a break!"

Steer clear of the usual smoking areas. Take a walk around the block, around the building, or just go look out a window at the beautiful or interesting sights there. You don't have to smoke to take a break — just take one.

People use cigarettes to reward themselves. Do some-thing different. Instead of a cigarette when that stack of papers has been sorted, offer yourself a foot rub, or a cup of herbal tea, or some time just to sit. Be sure to think up lots of different rewards—big rewards and small rewards. With the exception of a special dinner out, none of your rewards should be food. Continually look for pleasurable activities that can be alternatives to smoking cigarettes. Some people suck on cloves, the type used to flavor ham. Some chew sugarless gum and others chew on cinnamon bark sticks.

When you talk on the telephone, hold the telephone in a different way in a different hand. Walk around your desk as you talk. Pace up and down. Doodle with your free hand. Anything, just anything, to change the set when you're in a circumstance where you used to smoke.

After you finish a meal, push the plate away, or get up immediately and take the plate to the kitchen while saying, "What a lovely meal. I can taste things so much better now."

Decide to take a walk after your meal, or go build a bookcase, or polish your nails or your shoes. Get it?

When naming the times and places and activities people most associate with smoking, driving the car is always up there on the lists. Be creative when thinking how to change this one. It's not so easy to do things differently while driving. Have bottled water on the seat next to you. Take new and unusual routes to work or to the market. I suggest that people sing "You Are My Sunshine" out the car window at passersby. I don't know that anyone has tried it.

And if you have children, we can assume you did not smoke in the car as you were taxiing them hither and yon. If you did smoke in the car with the kiddlings, be grateful for the gift you are giving them as well.

As you begin your process and you make your own list of your strongest smoking associations, plan alternative activities for each item on your list.

If, in spite of all your planning, you find yourself in the middle of a strong urge which somehow snuck up on you, decide to count backwards from 100 to 1, as one of my quitters did. It is distracting and you will get bored and turn to something else.

Again, be creative. You will think of lots of different things to do—alternative behaviors, interventions. Have some fun. Take some healthy risks. Really do something different. Enjoy!

Strategy #6: Relaxation

There is a strong element of anxiety attached to the process of becoming a nonsmoker. Smokers are afraid of two things: They are afraid they will fail at quitting and they are afraid they will actually quit and have to face the world and the future cigaretteless. Besides this paradoxical fear, there are other fears attached to quitting.

Smokers are compelled to smoke because the urges themselves are mini- or maxi-anxiety attacks. The feelings of anxiety may either be coupled with the urges to smoke or, in fact, may be the urges themselves. In other words, the feeling that signals "It's time to smoke!" may come as a full-blown panic reaction:

"I can't stand these feelings, I have to smoke!"

Sweaty palms, burning face, racing heart, hyperventilation. The works. Anyone who has ever experienced a panic attack will tell you there is nothing worse than the indescribable feeling which compels him to action, even though what action to take is unclear.

Two effective ways of countering feelings of anxiety are *relaxation* and *physical movement*. (We'll discuss pharmaceuticals later, and we're not counting alcohol or illegal drugs. Not a good idea. One person told me he was smoking 20 joints a day now that he had quit smoking cigarettes. I suggested that perhaps that was not a suitable substitute.)

Relaxation and anxiety are opposite feeling states, so it's difficult to be panicked when you're relaxed. There are many relaxation strategies. Deep breathing is an easy one, as follows:

Inhale deeply through your nose, filling up your lungs until your rib cage expands. Hold the breath for three seconds, counting one thousand, two thousand, three thousand. Good. Now slowly exhale through your mouth. Allow the air to escape as though you were a balloon collapsing. Exhale all the air and allow yourself to become limp and relaxed just like that balloon. Make a positive statement such as, "How wonderful it feels to breathe sweet fresh air," or "How clever I am to be a nonsmoker and how nice it is for my lungs to enjoy this beautiful clean air."

Smoking Cigarettes

The deep breathing may be used numerous times throughout the day but probably no more than three in close succession.

Relaxation CDs and tapes that assist people in coping with general stress are popular and are available in book and record stores. You will find such a recording helpful in dealing with your anxious feelings. I have made a tape/CD that I use with my cessation classes. You might wish to create your own, one just perfect for you.

In creating your tape, use only positive statements in the present tense. Negative statements counter what you're trying to accomplish. Future statements like "tomorrow I will" may never happen. Always say, "I am'" or "now I feel" using the first-person pronoun.

You should offer some specific instructions, such as taking the deep breaths I described. Use a quiet, calming, slow voice as you make these suggestions. Do not be rushed or overly energetic, but rather, relaxed and soothing. Peaceful.

Use visual imagery, such as placing yourself on a peaceful beach with a soft breeze and swaying palms, or some place that you associate with being relaxed — a rippling stream, a lake. Water images are relaxing.

The entire tape should be from the point of view of being a nonsmoker. "How sweet it is to breathe this lovely air." "How relieved I am that I am free." "How wonderful that I am regaining my health."

Making your tape can be fun and interesting and once you get into the practice of using it, you will be able to help yourself relax in any stressful situation.

Your tape should be about 15 to 20 minutes long. Use pauses throughout, giving time for the suggestions about relaxing to be followed. Twenty minutes is long enough to achieve a relaxed feeling but short enough to enable you to use your tape a number of times throughout the day.

Chapter Three

After you have made your recording, plan to use it sitting up in a chair for the first several times. Later on you can use it lying down, but it might cause you to fall asleep. Some experts believe you will continue to get the benefits from the tape even as you sleep. At first, though, we want your mind to be fully awake to register the cues to relaxation and how your body responds to them. Never play your tape while driving.

Sit comfortably in the chair in a quiet room where you won't be disturbed. If you are needed during your relaxation exercise, you will immediately open your eyes and be aware that you are needed. But try to be in a comfortably warm place by yourself. If two of you are beginning the quitting process together, you can do your tape exercise together. The benefits will be the same.

The more you follow the suggestions on your tape, the more relaxed you will become, both during and after.

Strategy # 7: Physical Movement

You can also break up anxiety with physical movement, a physical intervention. Unwanted or perseverating (spontaneously recurring) thoughts and feelings can be interrupted by an intervening physical action. It can be as simple as snapping your fingers.

"Oh, yes, there it is again, that unpleasant feeling. Right now I choose to snap my fingers."

I tell people to march up and down with large dramatic steps to John Phillip Sousa being played loudly on the CD player. Swing your arms wildly around, dance, sing along, or simply stand on your head in the corner. Especially at work. Just kidding.

Ideally, you should leave the house, or wherever you are, and walk, run, or take a bicycle ride. (And notice how much easier all those activities are as a nonsmoker.)

I have suggested that people use the urge feeling as a signal to get down on the floor to do five sit-ups. Mostly we don't like doing sit-ups so if you do them every time you get an urge, you are likely to cut down quickly on the number of urges you give yourself. *Never lose sight of the fact that it is your unconscious urging you to smoke. So — you are giving yourself the urges. This idea can empower you to take charge of your urges and put a stop to them.*

You get the idea about a physical intervention. Be creative. Take some risks. Think up some far out ways to get in the middle and interrupt those unhappy feelings. Here's an example:

Imagine 100 fearful flyers in a circle at LAX. We were stomping our feet and waving our arms just before we were to take the graduation flight for our Fearful Flyers class. As we chanted, "We're scared but we don't give a damn," travelers from all over the world stopped to watch. As the 747 rumbled down the runway for takeoff, we were directed to "wiggle our toes," a successful physical diversion to keep our attention from our fear of the dreaded departure from terra firma. It worked. We all stayed on board.

Strategy #8: Mental Imagery

We hear a lot about visualization and imagery. Psychologists teach these techniques to help people become who they would like to be. For example, sports psychologists teach runners to visualize the race before it actually happens. The athletes are taught to visualize themselves performing at peak prior to an athletic event. It is apparently helpful and many athletes swear by it, certain that it enhances their performances.

We gave examples of imagery when we discussed how to make your relaxation tape. When you use imagery without a tape, find a quiet place where you will be undisturbed for a few minutes, perhaps before you get out of bed in the morning and/or before you go to sleep at night. Imagine how you look as a nonsmoker and what kinds of thing you will be doing. Imagine talking on the telephone without a cigarette burning close by. Imagine how you feel as a non-smoker, how much more energy you have and how much healthier your skin color is. You are developing a healthy glow. See yourself that way in your imagination.

As much as possible, go through your day's activities in your imagination — as a nonsmoker. Congratulate yourself for your cleverness. Be positive. Smile. All in the privacy of your own inner thoughts. Enjoy the prospect of being a comfortable nonsmoker.

Visualize going to visit or having lunch with someone who will be very happy now that you've made this important life decision: your mother, sister, a friend.

You are a nonsmoker. Practice doing that, not smoking, in visualization. Say no, thank you, in your imagination when someone offers you a cigarette. Ask for the nonsmoking section of the restaurant in your imagination. Make love in your imagination, without having to think about how soon you can get at that cigarette.

We told you about how athletes use this practice. Salesmen also use visualization to ensure success. You can, too.

Try to practice your imaginings several times each day. It can be as short as 30 seconds.

"I'm a nonsmoker!"

Or as long as 15 minutes.

"I'll plan my nonsmoker's day."

It works. You are defining for yourself who you wish to be, how you wish to feel, and how you wish to act. Be creative and trust in your ability to do what your imaginings depict.

Strategy #9: Counterconditioning

If you took Psychology 1A you would have read about counterconditioning. For example, if rats in a cage get a slight electrical shock when they do a particular behavior, in a short time, the rats cease doing that behavior. There are programs available to you which employ counterconditioning or aversion therapy to assist you with your desire to quit smoking. Stephen King wrote a horrifying but comical story called "Quitters, Inc." It is part of the book, *Night Shift*. The aversion therapy King depicts is quite creative and something you would never want to be a part of. You can see the piece in a video called "Cat's Eye."

Stephen King notwithstanding, aversion therapy is shown over and again in the literature to be an effective tool for shortening the time the quitter spends in distress. The interventions range from a rubber band around the wrist to be snapped when an urge comes, to a series of daily bouts with puffing cigarettes in a closed-in room in front of a mirror. Sometimes the puffing is accompanied by a mild electric shock to the forearm when the cigarette is lifted to the mouth. Sounds draconian, but I worked in an aversion therapy clinic for two years and the method was very effective.

I believe that a mild intervention of puffing can be helpful in the first 24 hours but even then, better used in a clinical setting. Interestingly, a publication by the U.S. Department of Health, *Treating Tobacco Use and Dependence*, shows that aversion therapy or rapid smoking has the highest rate of estimated abstinence. However, the publication goes on to say that the practice is infrequently used today.

I no longer use puffing in my cessation classes because there is never a good place to do it. I have taken people outside to sit around a table looking at one another, but it gets cold outside. There are no public buildings in California that allow smoking inside. So, as much as I believe in its effectiveness, I no longer use aversion therapy, otherwise known as puffing.

If you are still interested, you may be able to find a program in your city that offers this therapy. (You can find Shick-Shadel Hospital on the Internet.)

Or you can set up your own little aversion treatment at home.

Use this on or before your quit day. Sit by yourself with an ashtray and your favorite brand clearly visible in front of you. Light three cigarettes (do not inhale) and lay them in the ashtray. Pick one up and puff it, set it down. Pick the next up and puff, then set it down. Do this slowly, rest your hand for a couple of seconds between puffs. Puff the three cigarettes all the way down. Again, DO NOT IN-HALE, or you will become very ill. Just take the smoke into your mouth and blow it out again. Pfffffff.

Note how hot the cigarette and smoke is. Note how terrible it tastes just puffing. Notice that you are beginning to drool just a bit and your eyes are beginning to burn and tear. All the while you can think about the 4,000 or more poisonous chemicals that are in cigarettes. Acetone, arsenic, nicotine, and so on. Continue until you've puffed six to nine cigarettes. Light one more and puff it rapidly all the way down, leaning over the ashtray. Put it out with a statement like, "Amen, I'm all done with that."

Now take the remaining cigarettes, tear them up into a jar and add the ashes you have just created. Run water into the jar and note how nasty the mixture smells. You can keep the jar around for a few days just to remind yourself about how ghastly cigarettes really are.

Do not do aversion therapy after your quit day because it could become an excuse to buy more cigarettes, light them, taste them, and so on. This is just to provide a little boost for that first 24 hours.

Note: This strategy is not to be tried by smokeless tobacco users. Those types of products are dangerously strong.

Strategy #10: Spiritual Practices

Years ago when I worked with drug and alcohol addicts, it was clear to me that those who joined a religious rehabilitation group had a very good chance at recovery.

We used to say, "He got Jesus, so he got well." It is true, the best known and probably most effective method of dealing with alcoholism is Alcoholics Anonymous (AA) 12-step program, the center of which is a belief in a higher power.

People make their own personal choices about their belief systems and how they practice those beliefs. Most Western religious groups would suggest prayer as a vehicle for assistance in succeeding in whatever is undertaken. Eastern philosophies might suggest meditation as a means of obtaining difficult goals. I have a dear friend who is Buddhist and chants each morning and evening, keeping focused on those things in her life that need special attention. I have assisted people with all varieties of beliefs and practices. I encouraged them all because I believe that if you attend to your spiritual unfoldment, all earthly tasks become easier. People have told me that God brought them to me. Others told me they had prayed to be rid of their smoking habits.

My sister, who had smoked for 35 years, stopped smoking at age 52 with assistance from her Sufi teacher. It was indeed a miracle.

Seek and ye shall find. Ask and it shall be given unto you. If you want it, it can happen for you. Your spiritual life can help you in becoming a nonsmoker.

I have listed 10 strategies and interventions for you to use to assist you in becoming a nonsmoker. Those are

1. Negative versus positive thoughts
2. A support system
3. A journal
4. Countdown/cut down
5. Alternative behaviors
6. Relaxation
7. Physical movement
8. Mental imagery
9. Counterconditioning
10. Spiritual practices

The more of these you use, the easier your process will be. We could call this a 10-step program. But you might prefer a three-step program or a five-step program depending on which strategies you intend to incorporate into your process.

Remember, the more you concentrate and put energy into these activities, the easier your process will become. The more you focus on alternatives and planning, the less time you have to fight the will power battle everyone talks about.

"I will smoke!"

"No, I won't smoke!"

"Yes I will, it's not really so bad for me."

And so on. You are likely to lose that one. So focus on positive, directed activities to avoid the fight.

Each day notice the pluses that are beginning to accumulate as a result of not smoking. You will begin to breathe easier within 24 hours. Notice this and the other good things that are happening to you. These things will begin to reinforce your new lifestyle and help you become a permanent, comfortable nonsmoker.

Pick a day and begin! Clean out and dispose of ash-trays. Throw away your cigarettes, leave none in your environment. Decide you will be successful this time, that you intend to regain your health for all the right reasons. Be creative. Be positive. And above all, have trust and faith in yourself.

There are two more strategies to consider, diet and exercise, so important they get a chapter all their own. It follows.

Chapter Three

Chapter
— **4** —

Diet and Exercise

*"New findings suggest that eating fish
protects against heart disease, breast cancer,
and rheumatoid arthritis."*

Andrew Weil, M.D.

If I were to name one thing that might be the panacea for
all ailments, I might name diet (read nutrition). On the
other hand, I might name exercise. In any case, we know
that to be a healthy human, one must practice a healthy
lifestyle that includes eating the right foods and getting
daily exercise.

Diet

In planning for the start of your becoming-a-perma-
nent-non-smoker process, begin several days in advance
by changing your eating habits. For many people, blood
sugar is connected to their cigarette addiction. This is especially true of women because of their complex physiology.
Smoking a cigarette raises the glycogen in the blood as does
a candy bar. When you quit smoking, if you eat a candy
bar, your blood sugar will jump; then, in about half an hour

it will plummet. This low blood sugar can be a very strong trigger for smoking a cigarette. In other words, while you are a smoker, the cigarette essentially regulates your blood sugar levels. Part of the sense of needing the next cigarette comes from your blood sugar being low. We can use food to regulate blood sugar in the same way.

Now you see the need to eliminate sweets from your diet. I know, this sounds difficult, but after a few days, you will not miss them. Eating chocolates and cookies is habit forming. If you eat some, you find you want to eat more and more. Sugar is a carbohydrate and ultimately ends up as fat on your hips or stomach.

Thus, there are two reasons to give up sugar at this time: *blood sugar triggers and weight gain.*

Next, consider what else your regular diet consists of, along with your eating patterns. Do you regularly eat breakfast? Many smokers smoke and drink coffee for breakfast and don't have a real meal until the mid-morning doughnut (did I say real meal?) The first thing they do upon getting out of bed is fire up a cigarette and put on the coffee. Skipping breakfast is possible only because of the blood sugar consideration: The cigarette raises the blood sugar first thing in the morning, so the smoker no longer feels hungry and food is not necessary. If you do not eat breakfast, after you quit smoking, by 10:00 A.M. you will be having very unpleasant cravings for a cigarette.

If you aren't accustomed to eating breakfast, begin to do so now. Have some grains, milk, and fruit. Eggs are fine a couple of times a week, but forget the sausage and bacon. If you can't bring yourself to eat breakfast, at least begin the day with a protein drink or smoothie made easily in your blender. Here's a good easy one:

6 ounces of orange juice

1 banana

2 tablespoons soy protein powder.

And there can be variations on the theme. Pump up your immune system by adding a handful of blueberries or strawberries. It's a good, low-calorie way to start the day. I recommend three regular, balanced meals with lots of protein (white meat chicken and fish) and complex carbohydrates: whole grains, vegetables, fruit. For some people, to avoid weight gain and blood sugar lows, several small meals each day are the best bet.

The current thinking is that five servings of fruits and vegetables daily is optimum for good health and a strong immune system. Bright colored berries are especially good for the immune system; eat them several times a week. Berries are also an important ingredient in Dr. Nicolas Perricone's wrinkle cure, as is fish. And some of you might be concerned now about wrinkles.

Why eat regularly scheduled meals?

As you probably know from experience, if you are hungry and there is no food available, you smoke a cigarette instead of eating. It's that blood sugar thing again. Also, nicotine is an appetite suppressor as are most stimulants. Many smokers cannot distinguish hunger pangs from cigarette urges. If you become hungry while you are quitting, your hunger can trigger an urge for a pick-me-up cigarette.

If you eat three carefully planned meals or a series of smaller meals, it will eliminate some of those urges. A strong nutritional diet will also keep your metabolism cranking and keep your energy up as the stimulant nicotine leaves your body. Do not overeat or eat to calm an urge, but rather eat regular, planned meals at regular times.

Avoid caffeine and alcohol, both serious triggers. That is, smokers associate smoking with drinking coffee as well as with drinking alcohol.

Increase your calcium intake. Calcium is a natural relaxant, and most women over 35 should be taking supplements anyway. There is strong evidence that nicotine interferes with the assimilation of calcium in the body, thus smokers are much more prone to developing osteoporosis and other serious musculoskeletal problems. Some of these are disc degeneration, slow healing of fractures and incisions from surgery, and spinal compression fractures. Back pain from work-related injury is more common in smokers. About 50% of workers who smoke complain of lower back pain compared to 20% of nonsmokers, says Dr. Edward N. Hanley, Chairman of the Orthopedic Surgery Department at the Carolinas Medical Center in Charlotte, N.C. So take a calcium, magnesium, zinc supplement. Begin to repair those bones. You can ask your health food store about the appropriate dose.

If you are not already taking a multiple vitamin and mineral supplement, take one each day during your quitting process, and keep on taking it. And it won't hurt to take the antioxidants C and E, too. Again, talk it over with your health food supplier.

Nicotine is water soluble. Drink tons of water; six to eight glasses each day. Use water drinking as an alternative behavior to smoking. It washes out the nicotine from your body and facilitates cleansing your system of the other toxins you're carrying around after years of smoking. Some people say they don't like water. Odd, but if that's you, don't worry; soon you'll get in the habit of several glasses each day and you'll wonder what you ever did without it.

Water helps your tired liver and kidneys to keep waste and toxins moving along and out more efficiently. Have a nice glass of water on your desk or next to your chair, wherever you are. Try some of the lovely mineral waters available in stores or add ice and a slice of lemon and make yourself feel special.

There has been much research on the subject of diet and nutrition, and there is much to learn. Many good books are available in your bookstore. You have to appreciate that you have assaulted your body for many years and now it is time to restore it to good health. One of the very best ways is to learn about good nutrition and to practice it.

Exercise

Exercise is the other fountain of youth, the secret cure for what ails you, including smoking for many years, and/or aging. Regular, daily, physical, aerobic, and weight-training exercise. Chances are, you've abandoned all your attempts at exercise. The huffing and puffing associated with constricted air passages, clogged lungs, and poor circulation becomes very discouraging.

Find a physical activity that you really enjoy. If you enjoy what you are doing, you are more likely to continue doing it. If you don't like it but do it because you feel you must, you will soon quit the activity. Physical activity helps reduce the stress of daily life that occurs for everyone, even if you aren't quitting smoking. You will have fun and feel great, too.

Within hours of stopping smoking, your breathing will improve to the extent that you can resume physical activity. If you played softball before, you can play again. If you used to play tennis, add that to your activities list.

If you haven't been doing anything physical, start slowly. Walk for only 10 minutes at first. Hit the tennis ball for only 15 minutes. Increase your activity until you can feel your stamina increase and that you are really bringing about some much-needed repair. As a smoker, your metabolism has been, in part, dependent on cigarettes for getting going. You can accomplish a similar lift from exercising, and it's infinitely more beneficial. In *Dr. [Andrew] Weil's 8 Week Plan for Optimal Healing Power,* he suggests working up to an exercise program of walking 45 minutes at least five times each week.

Everyone talks about endorphins, those mysterious substances that give you a sense of well-being when exercising. Well, you too have endorphins. Some researchers believe that a good part of the tobacco addiction is related to the release of endorphins when a cigarette is inhaled. Again, endorphins are released within about seven seconds after inhalation. Understand that you can also release your endorphins by exercising. Vigorous exercise will make you feel wonderful.

In the Strategies chapter, we talked about alternative activities and behaviors. Exercise is a splendid alternative to smoking. Besides, you will be amazed at how much extra time you have when you're not busy buying, lighting, puffing, and cleaning up after your cigarettes. Use the time you're saving to exercise.

For people of all ages, a gym membership is wonderful. Join the Y.M.C.A. or private local gym. Let them put you on a program. You don't have to tell them if you don't wish to, but this will be your physical rehab program. If you have any concerns about how much you should exercise, consult your doctor before you begin. There is no doctor anywhere who will tell you not to get some exercise: Everyone can walk!

In fact, not everyone is able walk. If, because of a physical impairment due to an accident or birth, you can't walk, then move. Move anything you can, aerobically. Do it to music; chair dance. Do it in a fun way that gets your heart pumping a little. Physical interventions might be more difficult for you, but you can think of some things that you can do and they can be part of your ongoing rehab program.

Okay, everyone, exercise. Regain your natural vitality and energy. You can, and it feels good. And did I say, have some fun?

Chapter
— 5 —

What To Expect When You Quit

"In 1998, 44.8 million former smokers were non-smokers. In 1995, 48.6% of 'ever' smokers were non-smokers."

Centers For Disease Control
National Health Interview Surveys

So what happens when you quit? There are two ways of looking at this and two sets of information that you should have. They are the immediate sensations and symptoms you might have upon quitting, otherwise known as withdrawal, and the rewards, the wonderful healthful feelings that you will have as your body detoxifies and returns to normal. We will start with the good things for you to notice.

Rewards

What do you get for your trouble?

Freedom: sit anywhere you choose in a restaurant. In California there is no smoking in restaurants and bars. (We recently visited Arizona and asking for the no-smoking section found that a four-foot wall, open to the ceiling, was all that kept us from the smoking section. They do not know, I guess, that smoke wafts. (George Carlin says, "Isn't making a smoking section in a restaurant like making a peeing section in a swimming pool?) Take a long airplane ride without being concerned and uncomfortable wondering when you can have your next cigarette. Leave the house without checking whether or not you are equipped with your smoking paraphernalia. Take any job you are trained to do without extraneous considerations about smoking policies.

Heighten your self-esteem. Hear no ultimatums from lovers. No more wrecking your nice clothes and furniture with burns and mess from your cigarettes. Save the money you would have spent on the nasty things; for a one- pack-a-day smoker, that would amount to nearly $150.00 per month, and take a cruise or buy a car, depending on the extent of your savings. Make your lover, your family, your friends deeply happy, relieved, and proud.

As soon as you quit smoking, within two or three days, you will be able to smell the roses again. (I always get a laugh when I tell quitters they will smell things they never wanted to smell.) Your taste buds will come back to life! I remember having Wrigley's Spearmint gum after quitting and thinking it was the nicest thing I had ever tasted.

Many people have told me their sex lives had improved. We know that smoking causes impotence, so this improvement is not surprising. There are other reasons why this would be true. Pleasure may be enhanced as a result of increased vitality and also because of very much improved circulation. Or maybe one of the partners smells better and is more attractive. Who needs to know why? Just enjoy.

A few people notice improvement in their vision, again because of improved circulation in the small capillaries in the eyes. People say their hearing improves. This is because

of the improved circulation to the ear and because the si-
nuses in the head clear out as soon as the aggravation from
cigarette smoke is gone.

We mentioned the "wrinkle cure" before. Facial skin
becomes softer and nicer. Blemishes decrease because of
improved circulation, too. The accelerated aging effects of
smoking are stopped. The appearance of wrinkles slows
down, and skin tone is improved. You will become even
more beautiful or handsome.

Within only two or three days the biggest health improvement is the increase in energy level and ability to perform physical and mental tasks. People learn to believe that
they will not be able to solve problems without the assistance of cigarettes. In fact, their ability to problem solve is
enhanced when cigarettes are removed because of increased
oxygen to the brain. Many people report an increased ability to focus on a particular problem or subject. This is in
part a function of not having to leave the work to light and
puff a cigarette.

Physical activities are resumed. The ex-smoker finds
that pastimes that he had abandoned during the time he
was a smoker can now be resumed and enjoyed. Air passages open so that breathing becomes much easier, and a
little jog, before so difficult, now seems quite easy.

Let's return to the more serious health hazards associated with the smoking habit. As soon as your daily dose of
nicotine is removed, your heart rate and rhythm will return to normal as will your blood pressure. Therefore, the
Centers for Disease Control (CDC) say that the risk of heart
attack decreases within 24 hours. One of my clients practiced weight training, so even though he was a smoker, his
heart was becoming conditioned. When he stopped smoking his heart rate went from 83 beats per minute to 55. He
was astonished and so was I.

Chapter Five

The CDC also says that stroke risk is reduced to that of a nonsmoker 5 to 15 years after quitting.

There is conflicting information in the literature regarding accumulated plaque that hardens in the arteries. One woman said her doctor told her if she quit smoking, plaque related to her smoking would leave her arteries in about three months. My doctor-consultant said that plaque, once in the arteries, stays there, various advertised remedies notwithstanding. I believe that with proper diet and increased exercise, you can make those arteries better. Even if the buildup stays, it will not get worse if cigarettes, not heredity or diet, caused it.

The literature also varies in predictions about how long it will take your body to fully recover from smoking. Some researchers say there may be permanent genetic damage, that is, the damage will remain for the rest of your life. Nonetheless, the most reliable estimation of the time it takes for the lungs to improve, that is, to get all the harmful chemicals out and repair, is between five and ten years. That said, a client of mine was told by his pulmonary specialist that he would be as well as he could expect to get in three years. This is a rather negative way of stating that maybe it takes only three years for the lungs to return to their normal state. That is a bit more encouraging than the 10 to 15 years we often hear.

After 10 years the lung cancer death rate is about half that of a continuing smoker. This is not very optimistic, especially for a person in his 60s. And as I said, there is disagreement on these estimates.

Regardless of all this, lung function improves as soon as you quit smoking and improves up to 30% after two weeks. You will notice within a day or two that you can walk up the stairs without all that huffing and puffing you've been accustomed to. Breathing improves even for the most advanced cases of emphysema, and the advancement of the disease is slowed or stops as soon as the patient gives up smoking.

Eight hours after you quit, the carbon monoxide level in the blood drops to normal and the oxygen increases to normal, which makes you feel better and more energetic. If you quit today, chances are you will not get lung cancer, and the risk of getting other associated cancers such as mouth, throat, and esophagus diminishes. At least you will not be buying illness in the form of cigarettes.

Most important, within a few days or hours the quality of your life will improve dramatically. If you can get past the few days of withdrawal and the lingering emotional ties, you will be paid off many times in vitality, energy, a renewed zest for life. I promise. I have seen it over and over again. You'll look and feel younger, your life energy will return to your face. It's true. In just the five days that people spend with me, I can see a difference in their faces. On the first day, quit day, their faces are drawn and have an unhealthy hue. After quitting, by the fifth day the color returns to their cheeks, and the only way I can describe it is that they look clear. I am not the only one who sees it. The members of the classes can see this change in the faces of the other class members who have also quit. It is very gratifying and wonderful.

And of course, the recent nonsmoker is very happy about his or her monumental achievement. They are so pleased, relieved, and proud. For some, this accomplishment opens other doors. "If I can do this," they say, " I can confront some of the other problems in my life." One gentleman was going skydiving, another was seeking to change his career. All because they were personally empowered by winning their battles with tobacco.

What you might have to contend with, what you may have to go through to achieve all this, needn't be so bad. Every time you approach the process of becoming a nonsmoker, the experience is different. Do not anticipate what it might be, or just decide it will be easier this time.

Now you know what pluses to expect. Let these be your inspiration. With this knowledge and the tools in the Strategies chapter, you can do it. You're courageous and determined. You're adventurous. Do it. DO IT!

Withdrawal

In some ways I am uncomfortable writing this section. I don't want to put negative ideas into your head by suggesting symptoms you've never thought of — give you more to dread, so to speak. However, I do want you to know what to expect and how to deal with it. I also want to dispel some of the myths and misunderstandings you may harbor about what you have experienced in the past when approaching the process of quitting.

Firstly, there are numerous symptoms commonly associated with quitting cigarettes: craving, irritability, anxiety, restlessness, insomnia, difficulty in concentrating, increased or decreased appetite, gastrointestinal disturbances, drowsiness, headaches, decreased heart rate, and dizziness. You can probably think of many more. So much for the list.

Recall that the nicotine is gone from your body in 48 to 72 hours because it's water soluble. The primary result of the nicotine leaving your body is fatigue. Remember, nicotine is a strong stimulant and has kept your body pumped up for a long time. You may need more rest for a day or two. For some people this sort of dragging feeling may last longer. Most adult smokers do not remember what their bodies feel like without being constantly stimulated by nicotine. The new calmer self is strange and unfamiliar. The change may be dramatic. In older people it may take a little longer to recover, for the chemical balance to restore itself. The resultant low feeling, or lack of energy, translates to some people as depression. Your body may be some-

what depressed and you may interpret that as emotional depression. A few people will say,
"I'm so depressed and have been for days. I feel myself wanting to cry."
At least part of what you are feeling is physical, not emotional. (Of course if you are taking nicotine replacement therapy, this is all different.) Since it is physical, exercise will dispel these symptoms faster than anything. Being with supportive friends will be helpful. Also, make certain you are eating properly.

There may be a dizziness or disorientation during the detoxification period while your body is clearing the nicotine. We can speculate on why this happens. Your brain is receiving more oxygen and there is a resultant kind of rebound effect as your brain becomes more lively. You may even see things more clearly, giving you a sense of disorientation. As we said, some people organize their lives around smoking. When the smoking is removed from the day's activities, there can be a sense of confusion. The disorientation sometimes takes the form of being unable to talk correctly. At least two people have told me they were unable to form an intelligible sentence. Interesting. All this passes within three or four days. Just be kind to yourself. Take it easy. Sit down if you become dizzy (obviously.) During these days treat yourself as you might if you had the flu. Know it is uncomfortable but that it will pass.

You may experience a tingling in your legs, feet, hands and arms. This is your blood circulation restoring itself. Don't worry, this is good!

For people who have a blood sugar imbalance, quitting may bring multiple, uncomfortable physical and emotional symptoms. For you, several *small* meals each day will help. And be sure your meals are rich in protein and complex carbohydrates; whole grains, vegetables, and fruits. Don't eat any refined sugar. You may want to see your doctor if extreme discomfort continues. Cigarettes have regulated your blood sugar for years. Now you have to do it with diet.

Another physical symptom directly related to withdrawal might occur during sleep. You have, for many years, been sleeping under the influence of nicotine, a strong stimulant, as I keep saying. This has kept you from the deep levels of sleep experienced by nonsmokers. You may find yourself waking up several times with a start. Your body is unfamiliar with the deep sleep you are beginning to have and jars you awake, making sure you're not going into a coma. Funny, huh? But it lasts only a day or two. Soon you will be sleeping better than you have in years, requiring fewer hours of sleep, arising earlier, ready to go. If sleep problems continue you should see your doctor to make sure you're not suffering from sleep apnea or some other condition.

Some smokers believe their elimination will be impaired when they stop smoking. This because that morning cup of coffee and cigarette stimulate bodies to action. Choline chloride and pantothenic acid stimulate the cholinergic muscle lining of the intestine just like coffee. Go to your health food store and inquire. Or you can simply add more roughage to your diet. Like an orange and a grapefruit or papaya. Oat bran is safer than wheat bran and, again, eat lots of vegetables and fruit. Psyllium, the active ingredient in Metamucil, works great as a regulator of elimination. Also, drinking the six to eight glasses of water each day we've been talking about will help things get back to normal in short order. Elimination should pose no real problem to you.

So much for the purely physical symptoms associated with the withdrawal from cigarettes. The other things you'll feel are a combination of mental and physical/chemical changes in your body. A kind of reverse effect happens for a few days which gives the opposite feelings to what the nicotine usually felt like in the body. Things are coming alive again.

The Crux of the Matter

Together with the changes taking place in your brain chemistry, a part of what you feel during this time has its origins in the conflict raging in your brain. Your unconscious has been conditioned to smoke, no matter what. Your conscious mind has made the decision to be a nonsmoker and is determined to stick with it. The resultant conflict causes some of the feelings of anxiety, the distress, meanness, sleeplessness, tears, and short temper. Most of the strategies detailed in the Strategies chapter are directed at these symptoms. The more you follow through with the strategies and interventions, the easier it will be to manage the symptoms of the conflict.

If you do not reward these urge symptoms by giving in to having a cigarette, the quicker they will subside. It does not work to give in to a cigarette now to help the symptoms subside and continue your program later. By rewarding the bad feelings, you only make them worse. They last longer, are more intense, more frequent, and in general are more difficult to deal with.

Not rewarding the withdrawal symptoms becomes reinforcing. If you have even a few puffs, it is like a message to your unconscious that if it is difficult and unpleasant enough for you, you will allow yourself to smoke. Each puff restimulates the addiction and makes quitting more difficult. You cannot quit by continuing to smoke, even just a little.

After you get a few rough moments under your belt you can begin to say,

"Hey, I can deal with this!!"

The urges become less frequent and less intense. You are affirming the message to your brain that you will not smoke, no matter what. It gets easier and easier and the urges become a distant memory.

This is the crux of the smoking problem. These uncomfortable feelings have kept you smoking all these years. These feelings are of your creation and they will pass. Since you know they are of your creation you can, by working your interventions, help them to pass quicker. You're courageous, you're adventurous. YOU CAN DO IT.

Chapter
— 6 —

Spit Tobacco

*"I'm sure it doesn't help me on the field.
It's just a bad habit."*

Player, Los Angeles Dodgers

Of course, most people who use spit tobacco call it by other less odious names: chew, chaw, dip, snuff, whatever. The dangers in spit tobacco are numerous and visible. Pick up any brochure that offers quitting assistance to chewers and you will see the most hideous pictures imaginable. Gum disease, cancers of the mouth, tongue, throat, and esophagus, to name a few, all illustrated in these pamphlets. Painful, dangerous, and heartbreaking.

My smokeless tobacco guru, Liz Cofer, Cessation Specialist and Oral Health Educator, explains that there are essentially two types of smokeless tobacco in common use, snuff and chewing tobacco. Snuff is a cured, ground tobacco that is produced in three forms: dry snuff, moist snuff, and fine-cut tobacco. Chewing tobacco also comes in several forms, including the popular loose-leaf variety, plug tobacco, and the less popular twist chewing tobacco. The most common way of using smokeless tobacco in the U.S. is either placing a pinch of snuff between the gum and cheek or chewing the leaf or plug. The tobacco mixes with the saliva, and the nicotine (and other garbage) is absorbed through the oral mucosa into the blood stream.

The Truth About Smokeless Tobacco

There are many myths and misconceptions about smokeless tobacco. Mostly people think it is less addictive than cigarettes as well as being less harmful to one's health, making it an acceptable alternative to smoking cigarettes. On the contrary, when a user keeps a wad in his mouth for a typical 20 to 30 minutes, he absorbs two to three times the nicotine that a smoker would ingest with one cigarette. A dipper who daily uses a tin of snuff receives as much nicotine as a smoker who smokes up to three packs of cigarettes each day.

After using for a short period of time, a matter of days, the chewer is addicted, is forced to use the stuff more frequently, and has a difficult time quitting.

Guess what chewers are putting into their bodies each time they place a wad of tobacco in their cheeks. Tobacco contains over 3,000 different substances including pesticides, aldehydes, ketones, lead, amines, at least 30 metallic compounds, and radioactive polonium 210. Twenty-eight known carcinogens are present in tobacco (carcinogens are cancer-causing agents).

Nitrosamines are a class of chemicals that are allowed in small amounts in foods by the U.S.F.D.A. Several of these nitrosamines are known to be carcinogenic. There are more than 100 times the amounts of nitrosamines in smokeless tobacco than the government allows in foods.

And add to all this, high concentrations of salt, sugar additives, and flavorings to enhance the taste of chewing tobacco to help get 'em started and help keep 'em buying and using.

Doug Harvey, retired Major League Baseball (MLB) umpire and cancer victim, tours the country telling kids about the dangers of spit tobacco. He says that some manufacturers add minute glass slivers to the tobacco to help the effects get into the system faster. The glass makes tiny cuts in the gum tissue so that nicotine and the other nasty stuff can get into the chewer's blood stream and circulatory system rapidly. This is really something nasty to think about. We also know that there is grit and sand in smokeless tobacco which is abrasive and causes wear to the teeth.

Who Uses Smokeless Tobacco

Twelve million people in the United States regularly use smokeless tobacco. Ninety percent of users are boys and men in their teens and twenties. Seventy-five percent began before they were in their teens. As with cigarette smoking, there is an upsurge in use for college-aged people.

Though the majority of users of smokeless tobacco are men, there are also young women who use. They probably got started by having a male friend who used, or maybe they are in some way associated with the rodeo. It really doesn't matter why or how they began, they are just as hooked as their male counterparts. Women are more likely to be closet users because their habits are more an embarrassment to them than for male users. Unfortunately, new research shows a very strong link between breast cancer and smokeless tobacco.

Except for elderly African American women and some Native American Indian and Alaskan Native groups, use is low among ethnic groups other than Caucasian. That is to say, the vast majority of users are young Caucasian males. The highest rates of use are in the Southeastern United

States and some more rural Western states, with the lowest use rates being in the Northeast. In general, use is greater in rural areas and small towns.

There is always considerable use of smokeless tobacco among rodeo performers. These are romantic figures for rural Americans, and young boys dream of riding that bull or roping that steer while the crowds cheer. Hand in hand with this image is the imprint of the can of tobacco in the back pocket.

Chew and Baseball

Unfortunately, the group most associated with chewing tobacco is baseball players. From 30% to 45% of major and minor league players dip or chew. Thus there is a sort of using culture among this group that younger boys want to emulate. What the young boys don't know is that most baseball players want to quit, and 9 in 10 users say they know the habit is harmful to them.

There is a publication from the National Cancer Institute designed to assist baseball players in quitting. The name of the pamphlet is *Beat the Smokeless Habit: Game Plan for Success.* Throughout the book are quotes from ball players and former ball players regarding how they feel about their chewing habits. The overriding opinion of all is that using chew does not improve or enhance their ability to play the game. For example, Andy Van Slyke, Pittsburgh Pirates, is quoted, "I know it doesn't enhance my performance." Tim Wallach of the Los Angeles Dodgers said, "I'm sure it doesn't help me on the field. It's just a bad habit."

Mostly all this chewing among baseball players came about when the Surgeon General's report was released in 1964, and everybody knew smoking was dangerous. Players turned to chew, thinking this would be a safe alternative to smoking. In 1990, MLB issued a report on the hazards of smokeless tobacco and announced that it would be helping players quit, as well preventing young ball player wanna-bes from starting. Those efforts have not been altogether successful; note that from 30% to 45% of players use smokeless tobacco.

Understanding the Chew Habit

Chewers will say that smoking cigarettes and chewing tobacco are two entirely different things. They will further say that solutions for cigarette smokers are not necessarily solutions for smokeless tobacco users. While there are differences between a cigarette habit and a chew habit, the similarities way outnumber those differences.

The rituals are certainly different. For smokers it is about buying, lighting, holding, and bringing the cigarette to the mouth hundreds of times each day and disposing of the mess. For smokeless tobacco users it is tapping the tin, measuring the pinch, handling the tobacco a little, and placing it in the mouth. Do we put it in our favorite spot or shall we move it around a bit so one area can heal a little? The user works the tobacco with his tongue, spits, and so on.

Some users never spit. For example, people who are so addicted that they have tobacco in their mouths while they sleep. They may not spit if they are students or using while working, or perhaps, because they are neat types, they swallow instead of spitting. These people are ingesting even more of the addictive stuff than users who spit frequently so are more at risk for stomach ulcers or bladder cancer. No matter how much they spit, there are bound to be some tobacco juices that make it down the food track.

Even though the methods of ingesting the nicotine are quite different, the addiction is the same: the nicotine changes the brain chemistry which causes the addiction, just like with cigarettes. (See Chapter 2, "Why Can't We Just Quit?") This is the primary reason why once the user begins to use regularly, he becomes quickly addicted. For both smoking and dipping, there is habitual behavior formed around using, and using is associated in the conscious and unconscious mind with pleasurable events. These are the core components of a chew or cigarette addiction. The solutions are also the same.

Tobacco companies, knowing full well the dangers, continue to attempt to attract new smokeless tobacco users by glamorizing their products, portraying users as having rugged masculinity. With clever packaging and inviting print ads, the industry markets its products very aggressively. They advertise heavily in the venues where chew is most likely to be used, like rodeos and ballparks. In these same venues, they distribute free samples to underage chewing prospects although this is now against the law. Smokeless tobacco companies often sponsor rodeos, supplying prize purses and scholarships for college cowboys. Their banners are carried high by young people galloping around on horseback. All this adds to the pull for young people toward becoming and continuing to be users.

The Dangers

While the diseases associated with smoking take a longer time to develop, the diseases associated with chew can develop in a few short years. The North Coast Region, an organization funded in California to do tobacco education, produced a film called "Tragic Choice: The Bob Leslie Story." Bob was a former baseball player and at the time the movie was made, he was a high school baseball coach. He was married, and he and his wife were expecting their first child. He was 27 years old. He developed a lesion in his mouth, it became cancerous and spread to his jaw so that he had to have half his jaw removed. In a few months the cancer spread to his brain and just after his child was born and the film was completed, he passed away. His is not an unusual story and it is so sad. I have seen the film many times and never have been able to make it through without tears. A young man with a family. As he says, "It [chewing] was not worth it. It was never worth this. Where are the big tobacco companies now?"

The dangers are the same as those associated with smoking, except that they are more concentrated around the mouth, gums, neck, and esophagus. Add to these bladder cancer and stomach ulcers. My dental hygienist, Julie Willig, said that if you applied chew tobacco to the back of your hand and left it there as frequently as chewers use chew, you would develop lesions and cancers on the back of your hand. The truth is, it is easier to grow cancers in the mouth because of the nature of the oral tissue.

The new user will have bad breath, increased pulse rate, and higher blood pressure and will begin to have heartburn and digestive problems.

Within a few months a regular user will develop white wrinkly patches in his mouth known as leukoplakia. Some of these will be precancerous. His teeth will begin to have a yellow or brown tinge, and decay will be more prevalent than it would have been had he not taken up the habit. Gum disease and gum recession will also become evident.

What can be expected in the long term? There are 27,000 new cases of oral cancer in the United States every year and 9,000 deaths from oral cancers. Not all are chewers, but a good number of these are regular, habituated spit tobacco users. Not happy news. Ball players have reported mouth cancer after only six or seven years of using, and it is difficult to cure because its victims are young and it spreads rapidly. Think about our friend, Bob Leslie.

Besides cancer, cardiovascular disease is another strong risk. Though users don't realize it because it's not as visible as mouth lesions, using damages the circulatory system. This is about nicotine, so it is the same for chewers as for smokers. Tobacco users suffer 40% to 100% more fatal heart attacks than do non-tobacco-users. The salt added to smokeless products increases blood pressure, also likely increasing the risk of stroke as well as heart attack.

How Do We Fix It?

Here is where the issues of smoking and chewing converge. The solutions are identical. They go like this, simply put (and read Chapter 3, "Strategies"):

- Choose a quit day.
- Reduce your nicotine intake for a few days before quit day. Do this by recording and using chew less frequently each day or by buying and using less strong types of tobacco.
- Understand your patterns of use. Keep a journal of your use for a few days. You may be surprised at how often you dip, chew, or whatever. You will also notice that dipping is associated with many pleasurable activities in your mind. While preparing for quit day, be sure not to use during those activities. You must also make a plan about your friends who chew and how you will deal with those associations after you quit. You may have to spend a week or two away from your user friends.
- Eat right, exercise, use a journal, use relaxation techniques, use interventions of all sorts. Read Chapter 3.

A note: one of the strategies described in Chapter 3 is aversion therapy or counterconditioning. Do not try this strategy because the nicotine and other chemical content in smokeless tobacco are so strong that counterconditioning could be dangerous. The only person that ever threw up when I was conducting aversion therapy was a chewer. Ouch, was he sick.

Despite the fact this book is written primarily for cigarette smokers, you will benefit from the knowledge gained by reading it all. It is about tobacco addiction: why and how to overcome it.

I am quite sure, and I have expressed this over and over in the book, that while the physical addiction is a very real thing, your thoughts, ideas, and activities can overcome the physical discomfort. Determination, focus, and stubbornness will see you through to being a successful, permanent, comfortable nonuser. Incorporate many interventions into your daily activities. Use positive thinking. Ride out the bad feelings that will inevitably accompany withdrawal. In a few days or weeks, you will feel wonderful; the difficult times associated with quitting will be a distant memory.

Understand that the pleasure trade-off is not there. That is to say, for the pleasure received, you endanger your health and indeed your life. Having half your jaw sawed away is just no fun. Ask Rick Bender how fun it is to have half a chin. Rick is a courageous man and a well-known speaker who also travels the country telling kids about the dangers of chew.

As you have probably heard before, give yourself the gift of life. Quit now — or a week from now. You can, thousands of others, even ball players, have.

Chapter Six

Chapter

— 7 —

If Loved Ones Smoke

*"You know, our sex life has
improved dramatically."*

Wife of a Quitter (I didn't ask for details.)

A good number of people I've talked to over the years have been desperate husbands, wives, children, lovers. They could see the lives of their loved ones fading under the use of cigarettes. Most of these people were worried, but some were clearly disgusted. They hated the smell and filth associated with their loved one's habit.

They sought solution. Following are some ideas that you might try if you are facing the same dilemma. Don't have very high expectations. People make their own life choices in their own time. There are very few effective interventions to accelerate those choices. That said, children have more influence in these matters than spouses. My children nagged me incessantly before I finally quit permanently, and I quit in part because of their concern.

Things You Might Try

The most helpful advice is this: Tell your loved ones you love them. Tell them you are concerned about their health. Ask if you can be of assistance. Then drop the subject.

In Chapter 2 we discussed the bad-little-boy aspect of the cigarette habit. The bad little boy's back will be up very quickly if you nag, cajole, or insist any further! Now, if you are unwilling or unable to accept this rather passive stance, some other ideas follow.

Try a family meeting where household members gather at an appointed time to discuss issues of concern to all who live there. Having a smoker in their midst might certainly be considered an issue for everyone. The meeting should have strictly honored start and stop times. Each person should have equal opportunity to express his views, so appoint one person as monitor to ensure equal airtime for all. People can express their concerns to the smoker and offer to assist in solving the problem. Rules might be set about where smoking is permitted. Quitting strategies could be examined. All kinds of related issues can be discussed. Of course, this requires the sensitive participation and cooperation of all household members. The gang-up-on approach should be strictly avoided. Employment of love and care will facilitate the process. In extreme cases you might want to engage the services of a professional counselor to facilitate the meeting. This would certainly get the attention of the smoker, and he would realize this is serious business to you.

Ultimatums are risky business. Nonetheless, I know several people who have actually said to their partners, "Stop smoking or I'm leaving." Of course, the risk is that the smoker will respond, "Fine, may I help you pack?"

We all face serious life decisions. Whether to continue living with a smoker is certainly one of those decisions. We constantly make personal choices about what we want our lifestyles to be. If smoking or being with a smoker does not work for you, you can decide to take a different direction.

Smoking Cigarettes

Pretty harsh, I realize, but like the smoker, the nonsmoker in the family can make choices in concert with his personal needs.

If there are children, that is another issue all together. Exposure to secondhand smoke for children is extremely serious. The literature names many childhood illnesses associated with secondhand smoke, and as I've mentioned, recent literature connects Sudden Infant Death Syndrome (SIDS) with babies' exposure. At the very least, the smoker must not smoke in the house or in the car with the kids.

Another option is to buy a smoking-cessation program as a gift for your loved one. The smoker may feel pressed, offended, or angry. On the other hand, he may not have realized how important this is to you and may be very grateful.

Make him a gift of this book!

You may wish to enlist the assistance of an outsider. One woman had been urged to quit by the minister of her church. The minister had done the urging at the behest of the woman's very concerned husband.

Ministers are a resource, as are family doctors. Either of these people would be willing to participate in a "let's get him to quit" campaign. Professional counselors trained in addictive behaviors might be hired. Their main function would be to reassure the smoker that facing quitting need not be an ordeal. The counselor would give emotional and educational support to the quitter's process. Another family member, a beloved parent, sister, or brother might assist in intervention efforts, or perhaps a teacher or close friend. You probably have many people who also care about your loved one who would gladly assist.

Bribery is an ugly word, but it is not all bad. You might call it an incentive. Incentives are different than ultimatums in that they reward positive action rather than punishing negative behavior.

Chapter Seven

Elsewhere in this book I tell my own quitting story. My husband thought I would never be able to quit. I think it was his doubt that led him to offer me a car if and when I quit. He felt it was safe to offer, and the offer was made mostly in jest. I had a new Ford station wagon shortly after my last and final quitting.

You might offer a week at a health spa as a reward, to speed your loved one's recovery to health. A special night out or a vacation would be nice rewards. Don't promise See's chocolates, but your loved one might like a home appliance or a hot tub. The list of bribery tools (incentives) is endless, and with what they are spending on cigarettes, the sky's the limit. Think Caribbean cruise.

Scare tactics are negative and in most cases unsuccessful. I rarely use these kinds of materials in cessation classes. Smokers KNOW. However, most are in denial, and a dose of reality might help. Therefore, you might watch for articles in the newspapers and magazines with ugly pictures related to smoking. You can clip these out and surprise your smoker with them. Tape one onto the refrigerator, or mount one on cardboard and hang it from the ceiling. Strategically place it on the smoker's desk, on his pillow, under his car windshield wipers, on the TV, and so on. Do it with creativity and humor or you may have a very irate loved one to deal with.

You can devise a plan for an education week. Make a nice sign announcing "Education Week" and hang it in an obvious place. Each day have a new bit of information visible in a new place. It could be fun if done with humor, inventiveness, and tact.

Things Not To Do

Now, things NOT TO DO to your loved one who smokes.

1. DO NOT condemn. Smoking is a difficult problem.
2. DO NOT adulterate the cigarettes. Don't put bad-tasting stuff in them like parents used to put on the thumbs of their thumb-sucking children. Yuck!
3. DO NOT hide the cigarettes. There is a Speedy Mart on every corner.
4. DO NOT exclude the smoker from your will.
5. DO NOT poke fun, belittle, deride, sneer or try to shame your smoker.

Be Supportive

And by all means, if your loved one attends a cessation class or begins the quitting process on his own, be supportive, do not contest or belittle, saying you know he won't or can't do it. This may sound bizarre, but it is not uncommon for people to come to class and tell about how their partners have undermined their quitting process. Without going too deeply into this issue, understand that if your partner makes a significant change in lifestyle, it is sometimes threatening to you—maybe you will have to make some changes, too.

Also, if you are choosing to continue smoking and your partner is choosing to be a nonsmoker, please, please, please, be sensitive to your partner's efforts. Do not offer or entice him to smoke. Smoke outside and out of view of your partner. Do not leave your cigarettes and paraphernalia lying about for your partner to see (and want). Understand what he is going through and do whatever you can to help.

I have made a few suggestions for possible interventions with your dear one who smokes. Basically, there is nothing much you can do. Therefore, the most practical and positive way of relating to your smoker is to tell him you love him and that you are frightened by and dislike what he is doing. Be supportive, understanding, and kind. Smoking is complex and personal, different for everyone. Therefore, quitting brings varying degrees of difficulty. Educate yourself about the issue so that you can really understand it. Reading this book will help.

With compassion and love, give the problem back to your smoker to solve. It is his problem, his life, his life decision. He will, however, need your loving support. With that, he will eventually be able to do the rest.

You're Ready, Your Partner's Not

What if you are ready to quit and your partner is not? Truly, this is the most difficult situation of all. Quitting while being with someone you love who continues to smoke puts tremendous stress on the quitting process as well as on the relationship. There are established rituals in your relationship surrounding smoking. For years, you have sat together in the evening and while smoking, discussed your days. Or you have sat together smoking, drinking coffee, and reading the Sunday newspaper.

You rightfully expect your partner to be supportive when you decide to change a behavior that is harmful to your health. But how can the loved one support you in any way short of quitting himself? Moreover, how can you be supportive, understanding, and kind and give him his habit to deal with? It's a tremendous problem with no easy answers.

The best bet, if you can manage it, is to understand that this is your choice. You need to quit cigarettes now, external considerations notwithstanding. You cannot base your success or failure on what someone else does, on his behavior. You will need to stay extremely focused. Restate your choice many times. And you will have to let go of any expectations you have about what your partner might or should do.

This is your thing, it is very important to you. You are doing it for yourself, and you must carry on. For now, don't think about how he is injuring his health and well-being. Be kind to yourself; then, after you finish your process and become a permanent, comfortable nonsmoker, you can begin again to worry about your partner.

You may also be surprised. Previously I said that when one person makes a serious lifestyle change, the other may feel obliged to make some changes as well. Your quitting will conclude your support of your partner's habit and will, in the end, *be the best possible thing you can do for him.*

Chapter Seven

Chapter
— 8 —

Tobacco: From the Sacred to the Profane

"Each pack of cigarettes sold in the United States costs the nation $7 in medical care and lost productivity."

Centers for Disease Control and Prevention,
April 2002

A Short History

It all depends on your perspective. The ancient Mayas were probably the first users of tobacco. Their smoking habits derived from the incense ceremonies of medicine men and priests. Surely they saw tobacco as divine medicine, and archaeological evidence tells us that it played a significant role in religious and mythological folklore.

Tobacco was often depicted in Mayan art so we know that beyond ceremonial use it was used medicinally to treat all manner of ailments. Sometimes ingested, sometimes applied topically, many of the treatments were more ritualistic than practical. The healer might blow smoke at or around the patient while performing a dance rather than applying a poultice.

Probably the tobacco of the Mayas was several times stronger than that in use today. Whether used ceremoniously, medicinally, or socially, it was much more hallucinogenic than it is now. While under the influence of tobacco, these people demonstrated interesting and bizarre behaviors.

Before the Spanish arrived in the Americas, use of the leaf had migrated northward, and Native Americans cultivated the plant in what is now the U.S. Tobacco was known in the Mississippi Valley as early as the first millennium, B.C.

The conquest by the Spanish of the Aztecs led to the introduction of tobacco to Europe and England.

Tobacco was already a commodity for gifts and trade for the Indians and soon became such for the Europeans.

The first report of tobacco written in a European language is probably that of Columbus. In October 1492, he described in his journal certain dried leaves that gave off a distinct fragrance, brought to him by the natives.

Jean Nicot, a French Ambassador to Lisbon, received tobacco seeds from a Portuguese scientist, then sent them to the Queen of France as a present. The genus Nicotiana (tobacco) was named for the ambassador.

There are reports all through the 1500s of resistance to the proliferating use of tobacco in Europe. King James I issued a pamphlet that railed against emulating the behavior of the Spanish and the customs of the Indians. Too late!

By the 17th century tobacco use had reached China, Japan, and Western Africa. And in this country tobacco grew like shrubbery in the streets of New England. Becoming a staple crop, it spread to the deep south and as far west as Missouri. So there you have it, a few historical moments in the life of tobacco.

Smoking Cigarettes

Smoking Prevalence in the U.S.

In the mid-1940s when I was beginning my adventures with smoking, at least 50% of the male population smoked. The U.S. government encouraged its soldiers to smoke because it was believed smoking somehow relaxed the combatants and eased the terrors of war. Cigarettes were sold at a minimal cost or given to soldiers, and regular 10-minute smoke breaks were a common practice. Probably 30% of the older men I've talked to began smoking when they were in the military. Veteran's Administration hospitals have a very high rate of smoking among their patients. How could soldiers not smoke?

And the women, left behind to do the men's work at home, began to smoke too, just like the men!

Also, in the 1940s, rumblings about the hazards of smoking were just beginning from some corners of the medical world. These rumblings increased through the 1950s when about 22% of the female population smoked and 50% of the men still smoked. Young people were told that if they began to smoke too early it would stunt their growth. Of course, it was getting harder to ignore the hacking cough that was so commonplace among smokers.

The interest in the connection between health and smoking grew until the Surgeon General's Report exploded onto the American scene in 1964. There could no longer be any doubt, regardless of what the tobacco companies said in rebuttal: Smoking was a very serious and dangerous health hazard. The 1960s were a wonderfully exciting time, and that era will be remembered as the decade of social change in this century. Self-improvement, including health consciousness, was a part of that change.

By 1980, the number of men smoking had dropped to 43% while the number of women smokers had risen to 30%. When this book was first written in 1986, 36.5% of the male population was smoking and 29.1% of the female population smoked. The number of smokers (52,441,000) increased as did the population, but the percentage of smokers in the total population was dropping.

The Centers for Disease Control (CDC) published a paper in 1998 detailing smoking prevalence in all 50 states. Combined, the smoking rate at that time for adults over 18 years of age was 23.2%, 25.5% of men and 21.3% of women were smokers. Utah had the lowest rate, at 13.7%, followed by California (18.4%), Hawaii (18.6%), Washington, D.C. (18.8%), and Idaho (19.9%). States with the highest adult smoking prevalence were Kentucky (30.8%), Missouri (28.7%), Arkansas (28.5%), Nevada (27.7%), and West Virginia (27.4%).

In 1995, the most recent count in the United States, there were 47.2 million current smokers among adults18 years and older. That same count showed 44.3 million people who had quit or 48.6% of "ever smokers." By 1998, the extrapolated number of quitters was 44.8 million (103.8 million people had never smoked).

To the discouragement of health educators, over the past several years, the numbers of adult smokers has hardly changed, holding at about 1 in 4.

Socioeconomic data shows that about 33% of people below the poverty line smoke while 23% of those above the poverty line smoke. About 13% of college graduates smoke compared to 40% of those who only attended early high school. *Nuestros Recursos*, the newsletter of the Hispanic/Latino Tobacco Education Network in California, reports that nationally, Hispanic/Latinos are less likely to smoke (20.4%) compared to non-Hispanic whites (25.3%) and African Americans (26.7%).

The Worldwide Epidemic

In July of 1998, the *Berkeley Wellness Letter* provided a grim worldwide forecast for the next quarter century:

- The number of people who die each year from smoking will reach 3 million.
- The number of annual smoking deaths by the year 2025, if the trend continues, will reach 10 million.
- Tobacco's share of all death and disability will increase to 9% from current 3%.
- The epidemic will be transferred from rich to poor countries: by 2025 about 85% of the world's smokers will live in developing countries.
- More women in developing countries will be smoking—29%, versus 8% currently. But fewer men: 45%, versus 60% now.
- By the year 2025, the global tobacco companies will have moved their agriculture and manufacturing processes out of the U.S., and tobacco might not be grown here.

In 1999 NBC nightly news reported on smoking in China. There are 350 million smokers who smoke 10 billion cigarettes each day, and there are 1,000,000 deaths each year attributable to smoking. It is projected that in the year 2020, 1/3 of China's men will die from smoking. The income from all this is $12 billion each year to the state-owned tobacco companies. The cheap Chinese cigarettes are the biggest sellers in the world.

There are these kinds of stories from Kenya, Mexico, Finland, Sweden, Italy, and on and on. Some countries' citizens are smoking more, some less; nonetheless, smoking remains a huge health problem worldwide. As the United

States gets a handle on its smoking epidemic, the epidemic spreads to other countries.

Cost of Smoking

A CDC study, published in April 2002, reported that each pack of cigarettes sold in the U.S. costs the nation $7 in medical care and lost productivity. The study put the total cost at $3,391 per smoker or $157.7 billion. This is much higher than prior estimates. Health experts had previously estimated these costs to be $96 billion.

An earlier fact sheet from the CDC, "The U.S. Economic Impact of Tobacco Use," states that, "Tobacco use, particularly cigarette smoking, accounts for a substantial and preventable portion of all U.S. health care expenditures." The Office on Smoking and Health then estimated that each year smoking cost the U.S. approximately $50 to $73 billion in medical expenses alone.

The report continues: The most recent national estimates placed U.S. smoking-attributable costs for medical care at $50 billion in1993; with inflation, current costs are probably higher. The estimates included hospitals, physician care, nursing homes, prescription drugs, and home health care expenditures.

Public funding (primarily Medicare and Medicaid) pays, on average, over 40% of smoking-related health care costs in the nation each year.

And there are the hidden costs. Smokers lose from 33% to 45% more workdays and have 14% to 17% more bed disability days than nonsmokers. It is estimated that each smoker-employee costs the company several thousand dollars in medical expenses, costs for lost days, and costs for ruined equipment. Employee health care costs, in general, of which smoking-related illness makes up a large part, substantially raise the costs of consumer products.

Environmental Tobacco Smoke

Further complicating the cost picture is environmental tobacco smoke (ETS), also known as secondhand smoke, side-stream smoke, or passive smoke. *Newsweek*, in 1985, addressing the environmental hazards that cost everyone, termed cigarette smoke the "most deadly air pollutant of all."

Working in a smoke-filled room can translate into smoking 5 to 10 cigarettes each day for the nonsmoker. There are more than 4,000 components of cigarette smoke, and some of these toxic substances are found in greater concentration in ETS than in mainstream smoke. Tar, for example, the most carcinogenic substance, is 70% more concentrated in ETS. Carbon monoxide is 2.5 times greater in ETS. Nicotine is 2.7 times greater, and ammonia 73 times greater.

In the 1990s, government officials and company managers alike began showing concern for the protection of the nonsmoking worker. Many work places become smokefree because the business owners made that decision. Several states, counties, and cities enacted laws restricting smoking in the workplace and in public places. The comprehensiveness of these laws varies from state to state and city to city, with some outlawing smoking in public places altogether. For example, California, in 1995, implemented Assembly Bill 13 that outlawed smoking in all workplaces. After a three-year moratorium, the part of this law that pertained to bars and restaurants was also implemented. Thus, in California, since 1998 there is no smoking where people work, including in bars and restaurants.

And what about in the home? The 1986 report from the Surgeon General, *The Health Consequences of Involuntary Smoking*, reviewed the literature and presented copious scientific evidence addressing the relationship between parental smoking and respiratory illness among children. Hospital admissions for bronchitis and pneumonia are 28% greater for children whose parents smoke, and there is significantly more asthma among children of smokers.

As I mentioned previously, an article in the *Journal of Pediatrics* in 2002 proves the connection between Sudden Infant Death Syndrome (SIDS) and smoking mothers. There are two factors in SIDS. The first is the position the baby is in while he sleeps (he should either sleep on his side or on his back) and the second is cigarettes. Lung tissue from babies who had died was tested for nicotine. SIDS babies had much more nicotine in their lungs. "What was found there must have happened soon before death. Nicotine has a short half life," the researcher said.

It bears mentioning again that the 1986 report also says that nonsmoking women married to smokers have an increased risk of heart disease. There is evidence that demonstrates the same connection for the nonsmoking wife with emphysema and other lung diseases.

And think about those beloved pets that live in a home with a smoker. They are being exposed to ETS and are also suffering the consequences.

Of course the government cannot legislate against smoking in people's private homes, but health educators throughout the country conduct campaigns to help smokers understand what they are doing to their loved ones. In California, 70% of homes no longer allow people to smoke inside, and it is very common for smoking, even for those who reside there, to be relegated to the garage or front porch. (On network news recently, there was a story about a judge who ruled a smoker-mother could not smoke in her own home. Her former husband had custody of their son, and the son was bothered by the smell of cigarette smoke. The judge said if the mother smoked in her home, whether the son was there or not, the son could not come to visit.)

Tobacco Industry and the Media

In 1990, cigarette advertising and promotional expenditures grew to almost $4 billion, making cigarettes the second most-promoted consumer product (after cars) in the United States. This from the *Surgeon General's 1994 Report: Preventing Tobacco Use Among Young People.*

The Federal Trade Commission's annual report on cigarette sales and advertising for 1999 shows that cigarette sales fell from 1998 to 1999, but advertising and promotional expenditures increased by 22.3%. (In 1999, the manufacturers reported they sold 411.3 billion cigarettes domestically, which was 47.2 billion fewer than they sold in 1998.)

As director of a three-county tobacco education agency in California, for nine years I received information regarding the antics of the tobacco industry. As I said elsewhere, 44.8 million people have quit smoking. So how do the tobacco companies stay in business? They must recruit 3,000 youngsters each day to replace those smokers who quit and those who die.

How does the industry do this recruiting? By advertising that targets children, of course. In the 1980s and '90s, the tobacco industry openly targeted children with their ad campaigns. One of the icons of that era was Joe Camel. During the time that the cartoon character was used, in surveys with young children, Joe Camel was recognized and identified as frequently as Mickey Mouse. Ultimately, the use of Joe Camel and other cartoon characters was outlawed.

There were contests and giveaways and sampling everywhere. And in California, where a cigarette tax was

Chapter Eight

passed in 1988, part of which was earmarked for tobacco education, tobacco advertising heated up.

In the mid-1990s, a group of state attorneys general brought suite against the tobacco industry to recover the medical costs that fall to the states for smoking-related illnesses. In 1998 there was what is now referred to as the Master Settlement Agreement (MSA), where the tobacco industry was forced to pay $246 billion, over a period of 25 years, to the states that had brought the suit. As part of the MSA the use of advertising clearly targeting young people was outlawed, so there were no more contests or huge billboards depicting smoking as glamorous and adventurous.

Unfortunately, Campaign for Tobacco Free Kids (TFK), a private, nongovernmental agency that keeps track of how the MSA money is being spent, reports that three years after the $246 billion in settlements with the tobacco industry, most states failed to keep their promises to use a significant portion of their settlement proceeds to fund tobacco use prevention programs. As states faced budget shortfalls, they would use MSA money to fill the gaps, including funds previously designated for prevention.

While states are missing the mark in prevention, tobacco company promotional expenditures that affect children actually increased after the MSA. In 1999, the first year after the settlement, *the tobacco industry spent $8.4 billion, $22.5 million a day, on marketing—an increase of 22.3%*. The increased cash was spent on marketing in ways effective at reaching kids: advertising in youth-oriented magazines and in convenience stores frequented by youth.

In contrast, it is estimated that in Fiscal Years 2000 and 2001, the legislatures appropriated approximately $168 million and $430 million, respectively, of MSA money for tobacco prevention and cessation. (The complete report is available at *http://tobaccofreekids.org.* under Reports.)

And what happens in the movies? Thirty-seven percent of major releases portray smoking as positive. While approximately 25% of adults nationwide smoke, tobacco depiction in the movies has about 75% of the people smoking. In California, the American Lung Association sponsors a program known as "Thumbs Up, Thumbs Down", where youth monitor current movies. Each year, just before the Academy Award ceremonies, the group makes the Phlegmy Awards to the movies that contain the most inappropriate smoking.

More About the Tobacco Industry

Philip Morris (PM) and its cigarette brand, Marlboro, are household words, and to many they typify a loathsome industry. Thus, in the last few years, PM has been working to shore up its image. The PM company has run a number of ads describing how it feeds the elderly, shelters battered women, helps communities in trouble, and so forth. Just this week, the PM shareholders voted to change the PM name to Altria. But, alas, a rose by any other name, to quote Shakespeare.

In the midst of its good works, the company, along with other companies of the same ilk, have exported their deadly wares in huge quantities to Asia, and they have smuggled their products into countries where they are not wanted or with whom the U.S. does not do business, like Iraq.

Documents associated with the Minnesota lawsuit (see below) described the concern of R. J. Reynolds in the mid-1970s that they were losing market share to Marlboro. They discovered that Philip Morris was adding ammonia to its products. What happens when ammonia is added to the tobacco? The product tastes better, has a "roasty toasty" flavor. The big news is ammonia makes the smoke less acidic which changes some of the nicotine to "free nicotine," a form that is more quickly absorbed in the lungs and is felt in the brain within seconds. All this clearly makes nicotine with ammonia added more addictive. Reynolds began putting ammoniated tobacco first in its Camel Filter cigarettes, then in Winstons. Both showed marked improvement in performance (sales).

You may recall in1994 seeing the CEOs of the top seven tobacco companies swearing before congress that they did not believe that nicotine was addictive. In fact, these charming folks have known that tobacco was addictive for decades. (Alexander Spears III, the president of Lorillard Tobacco Company, at the time of that swearing, died at the age of 68 of lung cancer. His father, also a heavy smoker, had died of lung cancer years earlier.)

In part due to the good sleuthing of the office of Stanton Glantz, Ph.D., a California anti-tobacco advocate, and the Americans for Nonsmokers' Rights originally making them available, in 1998 the public gained access to the "Documents", part of 33 million pages, that confirmed what anti-tobacco activists already knew. A report from Great Britain's Action on Smoking and Health (ASH), "Tobacco Explained: The truth about the tobacco industry...in it's own words", contained 1,200 tobacco industry quotes. The documents were part of the State of Minnesota's and Mangini lawsuits and were further unearthed by some good Internet searching.

These documents are interesting because they detail what and when the industry knew about the dangers of smoking. They also contain memos of nefarious plots to subvert local efforts in California and other states to enact policies aimed at countering tobacco advertising and other issues related to the sale and use of tobacco products. And worse, these documents detail industry plans about getting children attracted to and involved in smoking. Remember, we said the industry has to recruit 3,000 kids each day to replace those smokers who die and those who quit.

The Web site address that will take you to the Legacy Tobacco Documents Library is *http://legacy.library.ucsf.edu*. This archive is a great resource to tobacco control and public health, especially for researchers, academics, and advocates. UCSF was funded $15 million by Legacy to create the library which opened in 2002. Go see for yourself. You will find the reading both fascinating and maddening.

Tobacco has gone from the sacred to the profane, from important medicine/ritual/social aspects to the most dangerous legal commodity ever sold. It is the one product that, if used as intended, will kill you. Though still used in sacred ritual by Native American Indians, the product is primarily used by unwitting victims who didn't really know what they were getting into. Most people started smoking or using smokeless tobacco before their 19th birthdays, so getting hooked on the stuff was not part of their consciousness nor part of their life plans.

You can take charge now, and take back your life.

Chapter
— 9 —

People's Stories

"Last time I was in the hospital I quit for the five days I was there. Then I got my husband to bring me some [cigarettes] and I smoked on the way home. Was he disgusted! I'm hopeless. It's hopeless. You know it is."

A Woman From Class

People habituated and addicted to tobacco come in all sizes and shapes, socioeconomic backgrounds, levels of intelligence, all ages. Very smart people smoke. Very rich people smoke and extremely poor people smoke, too. Cigarette smoking or using smokeless tobacco may be the single thing they all have in common. Thus they also share a kind of lemmings' death march. The illnesses they share are scary, sad, shocking, disabling, and terrible.

My Story

The first question class members ask me is always, "Did you smoke?"

Yes, I smoked. At the age of 10 I lit and held to my mouth wicker pieces from the white chair on my grandma's front porch. By the age of 12, my friends and I absconded with our parents' cigarettes into the citrus orchards that surrounded our small Southern California town. We coughed and giggled and had great fun playing grownup. When we were old enough to drive, we smoked in the car on the way home from the movies or football games. We sometimes smoked large cigars thinking that was a real hoot; we were quite clever and, yes, cool.

My beautiful sister, four years my senior, smoked by then, stinking up her room, her clothes, and her lovely dark brown hair. I thought she smelled awful, and I vowed I would never smoke, well, not regularly.

Nonetheless, I progressed rapidly, and at the age of 17, toward the end of my senior year in high school, I was smoking habitually. I was hooked. I think now I smoked to look older and more sophisticated and because I thought it made me more attractive. At the time, if friends saw me smoking and asked what the heck I was doing, I would respond that I thought cigarettes tasted good. I liked it!

One of the reasons that my sister and I smoked was that my father had smoked two to three packs of cigarettes each day since he was in his teens. We know now that the children of parents who smoke are many times more likely to smoke, too. Though my father smoked, he took the position that I was not allowed to smoke until I was 18. In the 50s it was just becoming acceptable for women to smoke at all, and I was still too young. (Neither did nice girls pierce their ears then!) Many times daddy passed the bathroom door as I emerged from my assignation with the cigarette.

"Smells like a Goddamned freight train came through here," he'd say, his pretty green eyes set in a frown.

On my 18th birthday, I sat at the table after breakfast and smoked with him.

I quit smoking at least five times. The first time by accident—it made me sick with my first pregnancy. But still, on the delivery table, I asked for a cigarette and resumed smoking as though I had never stopped.

Smoking mothers nursing their babies are a sight to behold. Ashes and smoke drifting around that sweet young child. Oh yes, I did it, too. I smoked right through my second pregnancy. God, if I'd only known; I still feel guilt. My baby boy weighed almost two pounds less than his brother and sister weighed at birth. He weighted 6.5 lbs. but should have weighed over 8. At two weeks, he had severe tonsillitis. It seems now, as I remember, that he was always sick. Croup, asthma, ear infections, every childhood disease. I didn't know then about the connection between SIDS and second-hand smoke. When he was two, in 1964, the Surgeon General's report was published. That was the beginning of the end for my smoking habit.

We lived in San Francisco, in the middle of the flower children, on a college campus. All of the married students who lived around us began to quit. Everyone knew they must.

My husband said, "Okay, I quit!" and he set down his package of cigarettes never to pick one up again. I was dismayed.

For me it was different. When I quit, I was anxious, dizzy, and disoriented. I felt really ill. Withdrawal for me was a dreadful experience. I invented all kinds of stopping methods for myself. I devised a countdown method that worked effectively for me several times. I was surprised when I saw a group on TV called Smoke Enders who used my exact countdown method. I bought a cute jeweled pipe and used it as a substitute, not too successfully.

I made a contract with my father. We would quit our cigarette habits together. We did. But I started smoking cigarettes again, and he began to use a pipe which he smoked several times each day until his death from lymphoma years later. I devoured pounds of See's chocolates. I used to say that each time I quit, I gained ten pounds. Each time I started again, I lost five. And start again I did. Once during a final exam. Once during a party. Once because one of my children was ill. Myriad circumstances got me smoking again!

My quitting process lasted fully four years. During that time, I loathed myself for smoking. Each night before I went to sleep, I badgered myself for my self-described stupidity. "Tomorrow will be the day," I'd vow. And tomorrow and tomorrow. This was a very difficult time for me. I thought I might be stuck for life, these cigarettes depleting my energy, ruining my health as well as my children's, the quality of my life seriously diminished by smoking.

I began to notice the heart palpitations, especially after the first cigarette of the day. My heart rate increased by 20 to 30 beats per minute. Some of the beats were irregular and felt like my heart was doing flip-flops in my chest. Doctors call this arrhythmia, often caused by ingesting stimulants like caffeine or nicotine. This situation really alarmed me. So after 15 years, at the age of 32, I quit once and forever my one-and-a-half-pack-a-day relationship with cigarettes. It was finally over. I was so relieved and happy that I don't recall regretting my decision for one minute. I never looked back with longing or feelings of loss. I would as soon jump off a bridge now as smoke a cigarette.

That's my smoking story. Now my job is to help other people quit smoking. Following are the stories of some of the people I've met. I've included some sad stories just for your information and some big success stories, too. Remember, I consider all stop-smoking adventures to be successes, especially since my own took four years before completion.

A Recent Class

The people who smoke and seek solution come to see me for a variety of different, very personal reasons. Mostly, when people reach their forties and fifties they are well aware that they must quit smoking. But the reasons that bring them to class on any given day are singular and peculiar to them.

For example, at one recent class, I had a particularly interesting group of folks. The group included a 20-something African American woman, Gracie, who wished to quit because someone in her family had been ill from smoking. Her young son, about eight years old, sat on the floor outside the classroom door waiting for his mother to reappear. He was also one of her reasons for becoming a nonsmoker. Gracie came to one class and did not return.

There was a gentleman, Sam, in his forties whose arm was in a sling. He explained that he had taken a fall, injuring his shoulder, and it was necessary to have an operation to repair it. The doctor would not perform the operation if Sam did not quit smoking. His former heroin addiction was obvious because of his missing teeth. He was an AIDS patient, also a residual of his drug habit. He was a nice-looking fellow, about 6′ 4″ tall with blond hair. He shared with the group that he had never known his family, and that he had grown up in foster homes and institutions. Now he was on disability and made a few extra bucks by gathering cans to recycle. His had always been a hard life, and while he was clearly in pain, he never complained. Sam was a successful quitter by the end of the two-week-long class.

A concerned mother had called me prior to the class, to get information for her pregnant daughter, Sheila. I explained to the mom that she should encourage Sheila to come to the class, and that if she would not, I would meet with her separately. Pregnant women must not smoke, I know from my own experience, and I wanted to help this young woman understand how important it was for her to quit. Sheila came to the class for two sessions of the seven.

Another very tall gentleman of Swedish heritage was approaching the age of 60 though he looked 10 years younger. He had smoked at a young age, quit for 25 years, then began again when his mother passed away two years before. He explained that he had been diagnosed with prostate cancer and before his doctor would treat him, he had to quit smoking. He was a good-natured and pleasant fellow, but as you can see, he had much on his mind. By the end of the two weeks he was doing nicely.

There was a married couple who had smoked together for years and who struggled and ultimately only attended three classes, to start the process again another time.

And there was a gentleman, Paul, also in his late fifties, who was a retired military man. He shared with us that his father had been a batterer, regularly hurting his mother. When Paul was 17, he and his father had a physical altercation and the father never hurt his mother again. Shortly thereafter, Paul left home to join the military where he began his nearly 40-year cigarette habit. Paul was determined and was also doing nicely at the end of the two weeks.

I tell you about this group to give you an idea of who some of the people are who seek help and to demonstrate that it is not an easy thing. People deal daily with all kinds of trauma and heartache. Some of them smoke. Those who quit make things so much easier for themselves. There are many things over which we have no control. We need to take control of this one, our smoking habit.

Others' Stories

Marlene

With curly red hair, round face, ruddy complexion, Marlene was vivacious and fun. In her mid-fifties, she was an office manager for a local doctor. She loved her cigarettes as energetically as everything else she did and clung to them after repeated hospitalizations for asthma.

Finally, she came to me seeking solution. Her doctor had given her an ultimatum. He would no longer be responsible for her care if she continued to smoke.

Like many people, Marlene was afraid she would not be able to quit, while at the same time being afraid she would. Because she had a deep emotional attachment to cigarettes, she couldn't imagine a future as a nonsmoker.

"I love to smoke," she told me. "I really don't want to quit. Besides, I've tried so many times, so many programs. I'm hopeless. I always sneak just one or two when I'm quitting.

"Last time I was in the hospital I quit for the five days I was there. Then I got my husband to bring me some and I smoked on the way home. Was he disgusted! I'm hopeless. It's hopeless. You know it is." (*Note her beliefs about smoking and how difficult it made her quitting process.*)

I didn't know it!

Marlene quit smoking in five days. She started again, called me and returned to me for further consultation. Hers was a rocky process. She cried in despair several times. She always had the courage to call me again, to continue with her struggle.

The first time I saw Marlene was in early June. The last time I spoke to her was in late September. She said she still had slips from time to time but was quite pleased with her progress. No more hospitalizations for asthma.

Chapter Nine

Then one afternoon about five months later, she came
into my office. She was all smiles and looked wonderful.

"Hi, Jan. How're you doin'?

"Marlene, I'm glad to see you. But you're limping. Did
you hurt yourself?

As we hugged, she said, "Do you have some time? I
have something to tell you."

We settled into some chairs and she began.

"Well, I'm not smoking, that's the good news. But I've
been in and out of the hospital. That's the bad news. And
in December they had to amputate my foot."

I gasped, holding back my tears. "Oh no, Marlene.
Why? You look so well."

"I'm okay now, but there had been clotting in my foot.
It shut down the circulation and the foot turned black. The
pain—Jan, it was unbelievable. They did everything they
could to save it. You know, I never thought I'd actually lose
my foot. It's still difficult to grasp. Once or twice I've taken
bad falls because I forgot. Like I'd get out of bed and start
to stand up.

"It was because of the years of smoking, of course. At
least the doctors say that contributed. And I was taking
hormone replacement therapy for menopause and to avoid
osteoporosis. Huh! So you see, you can't take hormones
and smoke, too." (*Neither should you take birth control pills if
you smoke.*)

"Yes, I know. But you had pretty much quit when this
happened to you. What about that?" I asked.

"Obviously not soon enough."

We sat together and talked for an hour or so and she
told me all about it. Trips to the hospital. Multiple efforts to
restore the circulation to her foot. The final dread decision.
And the road back. Her rehabilitation and how to use the
prosthesis, how to reorganize her life, footless.

Marlene lived through her tragedy as a nonsmoker, something she never believed she could do. She was grateful that smoking was behind her. She only regretted she hadn't quit years ago. Chances are, the clotting problem would never have happened.

Marlene was happy to have me share her story, hoping she could save someone else the pain and tragedy she and her loved ones had suffered.

Sylvia

Sylvia was a woman in her 80s. She walked slowly with a cane and huffed and puffed as she arrived at class. She had been smoking for a gazillion years and was now paying the price with emphysema. She knew that to slow down her disease and to avoid carrying an oxygen tank with her everywhere, she must give up smoking.

Sylvia was very game. She was enthusiastic about the class and about quitting. Sylvia was also very deaf. It was difficult for her to hear what I and the other class members were saying; nonetheless, we were patient and made certain that she understood what was going on. She chewed on crushed ice throughout the class, her effort to replace smoking.

"The crushed ice helps me," she'd say loudly. "It will help me quit. I always have some." And she did, in the thermos that she always brought with her to class.

Her story was even more complicated. She lived alone and had caretakers who looked after her during the day. At night she lay in her bed, alone, read and smoked, unable to sleep. It did not seem that she was frightened about being alone, rather, she had gotten into the habit of not sleeping. Smoking with its strong stimulant, nicotine, could only exacerbate her sleep disorder.

One of the rules of quitting is, "Do not keep any cigarettes in the house." The prospect of having no cigarettes around when she might need one made Sylvia so anxious that she could not dispose of the package that always lay within reach of her bed. We passed quit day, and she quit. However, the next day, she smoked two. I should say, the next night, because she did most of her smoking at night. The class admonished that if she intended to quit smoking, she must get rid of the cigarettes. I suggested she leave the pack in the kitchen, so that if things got too unbearable, she could go to the kitchen to get one. Even that caused her great anxiety.

By the end of the week, she proudly announced that she was two days not smoking, and the cigarettes were gone from her house. On Friday, we celebrated her quitting and her 82nd birthday with a chocolate cake (of course, sugar is a no-no, but it was a special occasion.)

When we met on the following Wednesday for our last class, Sylvia was breathing noticeably better, and she said she had not felt this good in years. She remained a nonsmoker.

The epilogue to Sylvia's story is that she was smoke-free, a nonsmoker, for three months. Her smoking daughter came to visit, and Sylvia allowed her to smoke in the house. Too bad, too much temptation. That lovely old lady began to smoke again.

Two points: Quitting at any age is important; one is never too old. And, secondly, no matter how secure you feel after you quit, do not allow people to smoke in your environment!

George

George struck me as being an odd sort of man. He was in his mid-fifties, a hefty fellow with graying hair. He worked as a freelance radio weatherman. He did not start smoking until he was 45, the oldest starting age of anyone I have ever spoken to.

George said he had tried everything to stop his two-pack-a-day smoking habit. He had read about aversion therapy, that it was generally effective, so he rigged up a sort of electrical cattle prod to zap himself as he smoked. The whole thing sounded rather painful to me, and needless to say, it had not helped him quit.

He hoped my program would help him, so he signed on.

He stopped smoking for one day. On the second he began to describe what he thought were withdrawal symptoms that were so uncomfortable that he could not tolerate them. He talked about a kind of tingling and buzzing in his arms and legs, but especially in his chest. He could not concentrate and was unable to work. He was also anxious and depressed.

At one point in our conversations, he told me he was hypoglycemic. After five days of coming to my office, his symptoms were so acute that he was unable to curtail his habit. I suspected that his taking up cigarettes might have coincided with the onset of the imbalance in his blood sugar. There was no way to verify it.

On the fifth day of the program, George was showing no signs of really quitting. I told him that he needed to consult his doctor and at the very least he should look closely at his diet.

I hoped George would return, but he never did.

Brenda

Brenda was a very attractive 50-year-old woman. She had not married nor did she have any children. She did, however, have a young niece whom she was very fond of. The niece apparently reciprocated her auntie's affection and they were fast friends.

There was a trip to Disneyland planned for mid-summer. On many occasions, Brenda's young niece had begged her auntie to quit smoking. It was Brenda's intention to be done with her deadly habit in time for the Disneyland outing.

Thus, Brenda was very determined.

She said to the class, "I've worked long and hard for my retirement and I intend to be healthy to enjoy it." She also wanted to live a healthy and long life so that she could participate in her niece's growing up.

As we got to know more about Brenda, we learned that she was anemic, requiring iron infusions. She didn't feel very well most of the time, part of her motivation to become a nonsmoker.

We also learned that she came from a family of very obese people and that she herself had been very overweight as a child. This always played a part in Brenda's thinking. If she quit smoking, would she continue to be slim and good looking?

Brenda quit smoking and was extraordinarily happy about it. Her health improved and she felt wonderful. Watching what she ate and joining a gym, she only gained a pound or two. Her niece was happy, too, and they took their Disneyland outing together, smoke free.

Theodore

Ted was a tall, good-looking man in his mid-forties. He had come to the class with a gentleman from his office where smoking was now prohibited. The two men were a little short with standing out behind the building in the cold and rain. They had seen my ads in the newspaper and each felt they had nothing to lose. Except...

On the first evening, Orientation, Ted said to me, "I have a problem. Next week I plan to run in the Bay to Breakers marathon in San Francisco. I need to train for the race. But I'm very interested in the class. Will you be holding another here again?"

I laughed. "Look," I said, "forget the training. If you quit smoking this week, you'll run better, faster, and longer than you have for years. Trust me. This will benefit you much more than whatever you might do to train for your event."

On Monday, quit day, Ted returned to the class. He had read the book and smoked a whole pack of cigarettes the evening before, nearly making himself sick. Thus, on quit day he had not smoked for 24 hours. Since the age of 17 Ted had been a one-and-a-half to two-packs-a-day smoker. He was one of the best clients I ever had. He did all the interventions that we suggested, and he participated fully in the class. For the duration of the class, he did not smoke again.

And it wasn't an easy class. One older gentleman with advanced emphysema had tubes in his nose connected to an oxygen bottle that rolled along behind him. A pack of Pall Malls was tucked into his breast pocket. He wheezed and coughed throughout the class. He was in extremely poor health and I would have loved to help him quit smoking, but instead, he quit the class before it was over. Facing not smoking was just too difficult for him.

One couple in the class saw a psychiatrist regularly for reasons I did not know, and they wanted to argue with much of the information that I shared with them. "Our doctor says this" or "Our doctor says that's not the way it is." Needless to say, these two were not successful quitters. Their resistance was intense.

In all, Ted and his friend quit smoking, along with two or three others out of a class of about a dozen. It was one of the most difficult classes I had ever had.

So you can see, Ted was the shining star of the class. At the end of the week, he came in casual clothes, planning to leave for San Francisco for his race after class. And he brought me roses with a lovely thank you note.

Chapter Nine

It is the protocol of the class to meet one more time for follow-up so that the quitters have nine days smoke-free to give them a very good start at being permanent nonsmokers.

At the follow-up class, Ted reported that he continued to be a nonsmoker and expected to be for the rest of his life. About his big race, he finished in the top 5% of his age group, by far the best result of any race he had run. He reported that his breathing was vastly improved, as was his stamina. Ted was a designer, and he told the group that the only really difficult time for him was when he was drawing at his drafting table. He said he replaced his cigarettes with a glass of ice water next to him and that helped.

The epilogue of Ted's story is that we have been a couple now for 12 years. We always tell people that he had the best aftercare one could hope for. And he continues to be, happily, a very comfortable nonsmoker.

Sally and Sam

Sally and Sam first came to my office with one of their old friends. The three chortled, making jokes, poking fun at themselves while filling out their questionnaires. They were wonderful people, good natured and affable, but they were in deep trouble.

Sally had dark hair and a pixie grin that matched the twinkle in her brown eyes. At 53 she was pretty healthy, even though she smoked two packs of cigarettes each day and had for 33 years. It was Sam who was ill. The first day I met him, he looked exhausted, his short, stocky frame wracked every few minutes with a severe cough. His neck and face became purplish red with each coughing spell, and his breath was shallow, rapid, and wheezy. His blue eyes were set in deep hollow circles. Sam had begun smoking in his early teens, and now at 53 he knew he had to slow his three-pack-a-day habit.

His was, in a way, a typical story. He was a workaholic, used to 12 to 14 hour workdays. He felt he had to work hard with a family of four girls and a wife to provide for. Meeting these folks gave me a deep sense of how we spend our men. We wear them out, as Sam was worn out, and use them up so they become ill and die prematurely. Cigarettes played a significant role in this tragedy; in fact, they were the primary culprit.

On this day in October, when Sam and Sally first came to me, Sam was operating on about 33% lung capacity. He had had several bouts with pneumonia and was still recovering from the latest. Emphysema was advancing. Both knew they must quit their habits, Sam for his health and Sally to support Sam and to protect her own health. Unfortunately, they had both smoked for so many years, neither really believed they could quit. They had spent thousands of evenings relaxing, smoking, and sharing talk about what had happened that day. Smoking was an integral part of their relationship. They loved each other deeply, and they both loved smoking.

They returned on the next Monday, quit day, to become nonsmokers. However, on Tuesday Sam came alone. One of their daughters had produced a child, and Sally had left town to be with her. Sam was feeling a little sorry for himself, he wasn't a very good bachelor. Nonetheless, he struggled through the week by himself and by Friday he had not quit, though he had cut down on the numbers of cigarettes he smoked. He was to return on Monday to start his program again.

That Friday was the last day Sam worked for many months. Sally called Monday to say he again had pneumonia and was in an oxygen tent in the hospital where he would remain for about a week.

Well, the story goes on and on. Sally and Sam became my best customers. Sally actually quit, but for five months we struggled with Sam's habit. He was 100% disabled, so it was difficult for him to do much about interventions. To make things worse, Sam's daughters all smoked, so when they came to visit, he would rummage through their cars for loose cigarettes. It was a little comical. He knew his family was on to him, but he continued to pretend they were not and it was a source of much laughter for all of them, including Sam.

Sam's mother-in-law came for a two-month stay, making things even more difficult.

Sally continued to be a nonsmoker, and Sam continued to smoke just a little, a few each week. Though I didn't believe he could keep his habit down, he said several times he knew he would never again smoke as much as he had smoked before. He had made his decision and was certain that he would stick to it.

As much as Sally, his family, probably his doctors, and I wanted something different, we had no choice but to accept Sam's decision. The last time I spoke to Sally, Sam was back at work part-time, and his health continued to improve slowly. And yes, he was still smoking—just a little.

(A Mayo Clinic study in 2001 found that levels of toxins in heavy smokers' bodies didn't decrease when they cut smoking in half. Apparently people smoked their remaining cigarettes harder, consequently sucking in more carcinogens.)

Norman

I met Norman in the hospital where he was being treated for alcoholism. Sixty-six years old, he looked like he might have been 80. He weighed not more than 120 pounds, one side of his face was more sunken and gaunt than the other. His bright dark eyes fairly bulged in his lopsided face. His gray hair stuck straight up in a brush cut.

Norman was a veteran of World War II. While in the service, in his early 20s, he contracted tuberculosis and was placed in a sanitarium. Thus he began his long career in the care of the Veteran's Administration. The TB had also set the stage for his future lung disorders.

When I met him he could barely breathe. Smoking up to three packs of cigarettes each day, he had advanced emphysema. He had been a street inebriate for years and though he was eligible to live in veterans' housing, he chose instead the freedom of living in cheap skid row hotels on his veteran's pension. He had never married and had no family.

Now he was unable to drink. His system had become so toxic that it rebelled after one drink, making him sick to his stomach. So he decided to take treatment for alcoholism, and at the same time, dispose of his cigarette habit.

As soon as Norman was released from the hospital, he came to see me. Each day when he arrived, it took him 10 minutes to recover from the exertion of getting there. He puffed and wheezed through his mouth, trying to catch his breath.

He talked about how he lived, especially about alternative behaviors as related to his cigarette habit.

"I went to Safeway," he said, "got some fruit and a little steak. I cup up the fruit and added honey. I'll eat that for a few days. It'll keep in the refrigerator. I bought a beef sandwich, half to eat now, half later. Along with my little refrigerator I have a hot plate to cook on. I can't carry so much from Safeway at one time. I get too tired. But the bus goes right by my hotel. It's very convenient."

Norman was bright and understood exactly about strategies and interventions.

"You know, I'm fooling my brain. When I want a cigarette I pick up this book." He showed me the book in his bag. "By Frank Herbert. Very, very interesting and I fool myself into ignoring the urges."

Chapter Nine

He quit smoking on quit day. The next day he reported he could walk a little farther without tiring.

"I'm amazed at how quickly I've begun to feel better. I walked all the way to the corner without stopping to rest."

Talking more about how he spent his time, "I'm painting in my room. I haven't painted for years and I love it. I have everything I need right in that room; TV, books, painting. I'm feeling well and doing fine."

His was a small world, but I was struck by how sweet his world became as he began to regain his health. Color returned to his face. He put on some much-needed weight. He was clearly breathing easier and he did quit smoking. For four weeks he continued on his recovery road, not smoking.

Then, as he described it, he found himself in a bar trying to drink, thus he began to smoke again. He returned to the hospital, then to me, the emphysema as bad as it had been before he quit smoking.

Again he stopped. But as he relapsed with alcohol, he began smoking again. The connection between drinking and cigarettes was so strong he could not override the triggers.

Norman was treated a third time and again quit. My hope is that this will be the last time and that Norman will be able to pursue his new and healthier lifestyle. His is a poignant story and I'm sure he wouldn't mind my sharing it with you.

There are as many sad and interesting stories as there are people who bravely begin to quit smoking. I have shared a few of them here. Perhaps you can relate to some of them. Understand especially that you are not alone.

Chapter
— 10 —

Where to Get Help

"For thy sake, tobacco,
I would do anything but die."

Charles Lamb, 18th Century essayist

How can you locate programs and products to assist you in your quitting process? You can follow my lead and do what I did to compile the information for this chapter.

The first thing you might do in such a search is to peruse the yellow pages in your local telephone directory, looking under "Smoker's Information & Treatment Centers." The Santa Barbara book did not list the clinic where I worked at the time of the first writing of this book, and it currently lists one acupuncturist, one hypnotist, and the now-defunct state-funded tobacco education program where I was the director. I concluded that this was not a foolproof method.

Next, I went to the library to look for books that might help my search. I was surprised at the dearth of information available there. There were many articles in periodicals, few books, and no stop-smoking program directory.

Still in the library, I picked up the Manhattan telephone book. New York City has every service anyone would need, or so I reasoned. Very few programs were listed for so large a city.

I then called the American Cancer Society, hoping they would have a roster of services available throughout the country. No, they only offered information about the programs and materials provided by their own organization.

Your local hospital may be of help. In Santa Barbara, a hospital, in partnership with Adult Education, offers a quitting program twice each year. Even though this is a promising avenue, it is difficult to know who to talk to.

In the three adjacent counties where I live, each has a public health department, and each offers cessation classes. Since the Tobacco Tax Health Protection Act of 1988 and the Master Settlement Agreement in1998, funds have become available in California for local cessation programs as well as the statewide "Smokers' Helpline." It is easier than ever to find help.

And now, we have the Internet. In this chapter and in the Appendix, I list Web sites where you can find all the information you might need.

All things considered, I have determined that by far the best way to get information is word of mouth. Your friend tells you he quit smoking. The next question is, "How? What did you use, where did you go? How did you do it?" Thus, when you begin looking for a way out of your habit and wish assistance, ask around: your doctor, your dental hygienist, your neighbor, and your friend who quit.

Following are the programs and products I was able to track down. According to the information available to me, I present name, address, program content, contact person, cost, and some notion of success. I discuss the pharmaceutical tools available and why and how they might help you.

I'm sure you would like to know if the program you're pursuing has a track record of success. I mentioned elsewhere that the relapse rate after people quit smoking is dire indeed. So, while everyone might quit during a class, on a given day, it's likely that a week, month, or year later, all that will have changed. The point being, it is tricky to assess the success rate of one type of program, method, or pharmaceutical product. By success rate I mean quitting altogether at termination of treatment and abstinence at one year. When making these assessments, surveyors don't know, of course, how much smoking went on between those two parameters. Some people consider drastic cutting back in the numbers of cigarettes smoked as success. Not I. For our purposes I want to know how many people quit!

Programs and Agencies

My Program

What I have tried to convey through all the previous chapters is that the tobacco addiction/habit is very personal and different for everyone. Therefore, methods of treatment must be tailored for each individual. That is why I suggest myriad strategies and interventions in Chapter 3.

There is agreement among professionals that a behavior-modification-type support group coupled with nicotine replacement therapy and/or Zyban is the most hopeful way to approach nicotine addiction.

I have written a protocol that includes those elements and uses this book and a relaxation tape that I developed for my groups. The program takes place over the course of two weeks and sometimes includes a mild form of aversion therapy. After the initial two weeks, there are weekly, then monthly, follow-up meetings. I do follow-up with people for at least six months with phone calls and an occasional mailing. For those of you who might be interested in facilitating your own cessation groups, contact us for the protocol at *www.joellepublishing.com.*

My programs have been presented primarily through public health departments and have therefore been free. Over the years, I have also held classes in businesses with a fee to the business owners. I have conducted this same protocol for 20 years with hundreds of people, and the vast majority, up to 90%, have quit by the end of the class. Beyond that, I have not been tenacious about ascertaining how many are still quit after one year. We're working on that now. That's my program. Following is information about others.

California Smoker' Helpline

This is a *free* telephone program that has been in operation since 1992 and has served more than 100,000 smokers. The Helpline is funded by the California Department of Health Services. The caller is offered a choice of services: self-help materials, a referral list of other programs, and one-on-one counseling over the phone. The Helpline also offers an opportunity to participate in ongoing research projects on a variety of related topics. There is specialized assistance for youth, pregnant women, and for smokeless tobacco users.

Dial the Helpline at 1-800-NO-Butts. Success rates for the service range in the 25%–28% levels, very good indeed. However, these numbers are for the people who are accepted into the program, and only smokers who have already set a firm quit date are accepted. This practice excludes quite a few people, so the program ends up with highly motivated participants.

American Lung Association (ALA)

Most medium-sized cities have a Lung Association office. Beyond literature, films, and videotapes, they offer three types of quitting programs.

Freedom From Smoking is their copyrighted booklet. It is divided into two sections, quitting and staying quit. The booklet is for sale for $7 in the Lung Association office and is considered a self-help book. For the person choosing to go it alone, supervision and support are also offered. For this do-it-yourself method, ALA boasts an 11%–21% abstinence rate at the end of six months.

According to the perceived local need, each office may or may not offer a seven-week group course that uses the same book. Again, each office decides whether the meetings will be once or twice each week. The cost for the group sessions is $50. I was told the success rate is 51% abstinence at the end of the clinic and 28.6% at one year.

And the third type of program is their online program that you can sign up for at *www.lungsusa.com*. This program is free and after you sign on, you will be sent a packet containing quitting aid materials. There is continued support online via a chat room or e-mail connection with counselors at the Lung Association offices. The abstinence at the end of six months is 25%.

The telephone number and address of the national ALA office is

212-315-8700
61 Broadway Avenue
New York, NY 10019-4374

American Cancer Society (ACS)

Most communities in the United States also have a local Cancer Society office. The ACS provides literature, posters, videotapes, and films relevant to tobacco use. They have some excellent literature on the prevalence of smoking among adults as well as among teens. They also provide trained representatives to facilitate smoking-cessation classes in the communities. Currently, their emphasis is on youth and families. They have a new program, titled "Fresh Start Family," for pregnant women and parents who smoke. This program also targets medical doctors, giving them tools with which to deal with their smoker patients. ACS cessation programs are free.

The ACS also sponsors "The Great American Smokeout" (GAS) in November each year. Well publicized, GAS is designated as a smoke-free day, and smokers are asked to abstain just for those 24 hours. ACS people say 33% of all smokers participate, and 10% abstain from cigarettes permanently. There is a youth aspect to this day called the Great American Smoke Scream, where, at a designated time, all the kids at a school scream loudly at once. The day is also used to present a variety of on-campus antismoking skits and activities, and materials are distributed.

The telephone number and address of the national ACS office is

800-ACS-2345
1599 Clifton Road, NE
Atlanta, GA 30329

SmokeStoppers

Their Web site reports that the One-Day-at-a-Time SmokeStoppers Program is the result of more than 20 years of real-life experience with nearly two million smokers!

The program is divided into three phases, totaling 21 days: Countdown, Learning To Stop, and Staying Smoke-Free. Each day has a customized "Action Plan" designed to help smokers quit one day at a time. The Web site lists a number of corporations where they have conducted stop-smoking programs, and they offer community-based programs as well. I could see no phone number on the Web site, but they invite you to enroll in the program online for $39.00. The Web site address is *www.smokestoppers.com.* There was no discussion regarding the success rate of the two million smokers with whom they have worked.

SmokEnders

Their Web site tells us that the National Cancer Institute calls SmokEnders the most successful program of its kind. (When I was quitting, I devised a quitting plan, then saw the same process on TV with SmokEnders. That was in 1969, so they really have been around a long time.)

They say that "No other smoking cessation program combines the elimination of the addiction to nicotine, with the psychology of breaking a habit." They also say that their program is endorsed by the National Association of Managed Care Physicians.

The cost for the seminar for individuals is $395. The cost for corporate seminars is $250 to $295, depending on the number of employees who attend.

They claim to have the best success rate. "A random sample of seminar records of 95,000 smokers who started the program showed that 81% successfully completed the program and quit smoking. Of 4,000 graduates who recently responded to a survey, 84% indicated that they were still not smoking one year after completing the program."

Not to pick a fight with these numbers, but most programs will have about 80% who finish the program and quit at the end. The problem is relapse. Of course, they are not telling us how many surveys they circulated to get 4,000 to respond. Guess what. The people most likely to respond are those who quit; the others are off feeling badly and ashamed somewhere. If these numbers really reflected the quit rate, we would have found our magic bullet.

Chapter Ten

Nonetheless, this is a reputable group that offers the components that are found in all good programs. I probably did not look close enough, but I did not figure out how to contact them. Their Web site is *www.smokenders.com.*

Schick Shadel

Schick is probably the oldest and best known of the aversion therapy/counterconditioning programs. There used to be hospitals and quit-smoking centers in Southern California as well as some in Texas and Seattle. I worked at a center in Santa Barbara years ago, my first real foray into smoking cessation. It was/is a good program, based on solid scientific information. Now they are located exclusively in Seattle, Washington.

Designed for individuals rather than groups, the program requires minimum attendance of one hour each day for five consecutive days. There is also a six-day countdown prior to the five days and a six-week follow-up.

The treatment consists of sitting in a not-well-ventilated room, puffing cigarettes under the direction of a therapist. The client is instructed to take care not to inhale. At the same time, the smoker receives a mild electrical impulse (shock) to his forearm each time he brings the cigarette to his mouth. The impulse is provided by a nine-volt battery so is quite safe.

The educational aspects of the program focus on the nature of the tobacco habit. There is little discussion about the hazards of smoking. Emotional support is ongoing, both during the intensive five days of treatment and in follow-up groups for six weeks following treatment.

I am not certain what the cost is; there is a sales mentality that precludes telling the cost on the telephone. However, an educated guess would be somewhere between $650 and $800. It could be more. The company occasionally runs specials. If cessation from smoking is not accomplished by the fifth day of therapy, the client may ask for a total refund of his money. As far as I was able to discover, this was the only program offering any type of guarantee.

Ninety to 92% of the participants quit smoking at the end of the five days of counterconditioning. After one year, the company says, the abstinence figures vary from 55% to 70% depending in part on how faithful the quitter is in attending follow-up. Of course the down side of this program is that it is expensive and is now available only in the Seattle area. Schick can be reached at 1-800-272-8464. See their Web site at *www.shickshadel.com.*

Others

When doing a search on "quit smoking" or "tobacco" on the Internet, I came up with lots and lots of sites that gave assistance. I found one that listed all the helping agencies in Calgery, Canada, one in England, one in a small California county, and so on. For example, in the first edition of this book, I described a program called the Cadwalder Smoking Cessation Program. There was a woman in Santa Barbara who offered this program, so I included it in the book. In my current search, I found the Cadwalder Behavioral Center on a site for Harris County [Texas] Public Health Tobacco Education Program, along with a lot of other available programs for quitting. The point is, you will probably be able to locate programs that provide services specific to the geographic area where you live. The most promising way to find them is the Web site of your county health department. Or simply give them a call.

Pharmacotherapies

As I have discussed before, the best hope for approaching the complex task of quitting cigarettes is a combination of strategies. While the pharmaceutical aids can be extremely helpful, there is little indication they work well without intense (that is, frequent) support/behavioral-group participation. None of the medications below will do anything for anyone without personal determination and a change in habit and lifestyle.

Zyban

Myth has is that Bupropion was administered to depressed patients, and among those patients who smoked, a number of them quit. It was supposedly quite accidental. In fact, Dr. Linda Ferry, who works at a Veteran's Administration medical center, not believing in nicotine replacement therapy (NRT), searched for an alternative.

It is well known that there is a connection between depression and smoking so that smoking can be a kind of self-medication for depressed people. We're not sure which came first, the smoking or the depression, because there is much evidence that smoking causes the disruption of certain neurotransmitters. In any case, Dr. Ferry, in discussions with psychiatrists, psychologists, and pharmacologists, found that Bupropion was an antidepressant that works on the neurotransmitters associated with nicotine addiction. Dr. Ferry was certain she was on to something, and with a small grant from Loma Linda University, did a two-year trial, testing the efficacy of Bupropion as an agent to assist in cessation from nicotine addiction. At the end of the study, all of the placebo subjects had relapsed, but 55% of the Buproprion subjects had quit smoking. In 1997 the FDA approved Brupropion, under the name Zyban, for smoking cessation.

Zyban is a prescription drug, and the quitter's physician takes primary responsibility for screening the patient as an acceptable candidate to use it. Zyban should be taken for a least one week prior to your scheduled quit date. There are a few contraindications that are printed on the packaging, and your doctor will know what they are, too. It is suggested that Zyban be taken for 7 to 12 weeks but that time may be extended to up to six months.

The U.S. Department of Health and Human Services book, *Clinical Practice Guideline: Treating Tobacco Use and Dependence*, gives the estimated abstinence rate as 30.5%. Online at *www.amerimedrx.com*, Zyban is listed at 30/150 mg tabs for $119. At Costco it's $98 for 60, and in general expect to pay from $98 to $135 for 60. That's not cheap, but of course the cost of cigarettes...

Nicotine Replacement Therapies (NRT)

The Canadian Council on Tobacco reviews the literature regarding NRTs and their efficacy in a recent article titled, "Nicotine Replacement Therapies in Smoking Cessation." Absolute quit rates are modest, generally in the range of 13% to 18%, about double the 7% success rate of quitters without any assistance. The quit rates shown for these products in *Clinical Practice Guideline: Treating Tobacco Use and Dependence* range from 17.7 % to 23.7%.

The accessibility and use of NRTs has increased since these medications became available on a nonprescription basis. The over-the-counter sale of patches began in July of 1996.

All NRTs carry the same caveat—YOU MUST NOT SMOKE WHILE USING THEM. Nicotine is a strong chemical and using these remedies while continuing to smoke could cause nicotine overdose with serious complications.

Nicotine Polacrilex

Okay, this is what the pharmaceutical types call *nicotine gum*. This was approved as an aid to smoking cessation in a 2-mg dose in 1984 and in a 4-mg dose in 1994. Chewing the gum releases the nicotine, which is absorbed through the buccal mucosa. Nicotine gum is sold over the counter at most pharmacies. The package insert tells the quitter to use the gum as needed, with the constraint that they not exceed a daily dose of 20 pieces of 4mg gum or 30 pieces of 2mg gum.

The purpose of the gum is to relieve withdrawal symptoms and cravings. The gum, online, is advertised at $25.99 for 105 pieces of the 2mg dose and $26.99 for 105 pieces of the 4mg dose, at www.buynicoretteonline.com.

Problem is—I have heard many, many stories about how this product has been used inappropriately. I have a friend who has used the gum for years as an alternative to smoking where smoking is not allowed. I believe from time to time she fools herself into thinking she is trying to quit, but the smoking continues. She has had one breast removed due to breast cancer. I have heard many stories about people who have become addicted to the gum and have continued its use long after the cigarette habit has been gone. These people have as difficult a time giving up the gum as they did the cigarettes, though I don't believe anyone would argue that the gum is anywhere near as harmful as smoking.

The caveat, then, in using this product is that you have a smoking quit date and a gum quit date, say six weeks past the date when abstinence began.

Transdermal Nicotine

In 1991 the FDA approved the use of transdermal nicotine patches as an aid to smoking cessation. The patches contain a reservoir of nicotine that diffuses through the skin and into the wearer's bloodstream at a constant rate. Quitters are instructed to apply one patch each day. There are three available doses, and the dose is contingent upon the number of cigarettes the smoker smokes each day. The efficacy of the patch has been tested in many studies with the conclusion being that the patch is an effective aid to smoking cessation.

The nicotine patch generally reduces overall nicotine withdrawal discomfort by reducing the craving for cigarettes. One study showed that the patch reliably reduced craving, anxiety, and irritability but did not alleviate depressed mood, restlessness, or sleep disruption. The authors of this study noted that with or without the patch, most withdrawal symptoms disappeared within three to four weeks.

Side effects of the patch are fairly mild; less than 5% of patients need to discontinue the therapy. The side effects reported are minor skin irritation at the patch site (30% - 50% of users), which can be relieved by moving the patch to another site. Insomnia is experienced by 1% to 23% of users. Other infrequently reported effects are headache, dizziness, fatigue, gastrointestinal distress, sweating, limb pain, and palpitations.

This seems to me to be a preferable NRT to the gum because the dose is regulated and the risk of getting hooked on the patch is less than on the gum. I have, however, heard of one person whose doctor kept her on the patch for over a year. If the instructions on the package are followed, there will be a progressive step down in dosage, so that quitting using the patch will take place easily in a few weeks.

One of the problems with this therapy is that it is rather expensive, about $60 per box—two or three weeks' supply. But at $5 per pack of cigarettes, after six days of not smoking, the patches are paid for.

Nicotine Inhaler

The nicotine inhaler was approved for prescription use by the FDA in May of 1997. The inhaler consists of a plastic tube, resembling a cigarette holder, that contains a cartridge or plug impregnated with nicotine. Menthol is added to the cartridge to reduce throat irritation. Smokers are instructed to puff on the inhaler as they would on a cigarette.

Since the inhaler is the newest of replacement therapies, there is not as much research available as on the other NRTs. Two studies showed that active inhaler use was associated with decreased craving during the first several days of the quit attempt but not thereafter. Another study found no effects of active inhalers on withdrawal symptoms other than on craving. Thus, it may be that the inhaler is most helpful for producing initial abstinence and that additional interventions may be needed to prevent relapse.

There are contraindications with the use of the inhaler, and the doctor will know what those are. The product costs $42 for 40 cartridges. A dose consists of a puff, and each cartridge delivers 4mg of nicotine over 80 inhalations. Recommended dosage is 6 to16 cartridges each day.

I talked to my friend Jane, a member of one of my classes. She as well as some of her friends had used this product. She said that neither she nor her friends ever came close to using the prescribed dosage. Jane used the product for about eight days, then began to want a real cigarette. She also told me that one friend still, after six months, occasionally had a puff, but she had not used up her initial package and she was not smoking. She only had a puff when she felt she "really needed a cigarette."

The downside of this product, in my opinion, is that it too closely mimics the habit of bringing the cigarette to one's mouth, a habit we are trying to overcome. I prefer, again, the patch and its nicotine delivery system, since it allows behavioral interventions to be implemented while it's being used.

Other Products

There are other pharmaceuticals, none of which I have seen or recommend. They include nasal spray and lozenges, both NRTs, and Clonidine and Nortriptyline, both taken orally. You may ask your physician about the efficacy of these medicines.

Treatments and Other Aids

Acupuncture

One of my class members wanted me to be certain to include acupuncture as a stop-smoking strategy. I am happy to do that because I know there are lots of people who benefit from this type of treatment. Nonetheless, there is no real evidence that acupuncture in and of itself, without other strategies, can get you to stop smoking. Information to the contrary is primarily anecdotal.

I assume that, like me, most Westerners have little knowledge of Oriental medicine, yet acupuncture is widely used in this country as a method of smoking cessation. The following information was given to me for the first writing of this book by a respected Santa Barbara acupuncturist, Roger Jahnke, O.M.D.

The conceptual basis of acupuncture has been part of Chinese culture for 5,000 or more years. The concepts were crystallized about 2,000 years ago, around the time that Hippocrates clarified the theoretical framework of Western medicine. According to the Eastern concepts, the cosmos consists of opposing but complementary energies, yin and yang. This energy is the life force and is inherent in all things, including humans. There is a constant movement toward balance between the two forces. In achieving balance, analogous to homeostasis in Western terms, everything is at its optimum function, all is right with the world.

But there is constant ebb and flow of these energies, so balance is always in a state of flux.

Acupuncture facilitates the balancing of these energies. The energies pass through the body through certain pathways or meridians. When acupuncture needles are placed at strategic points along the pathways, they facilitate the flow of energy that may be blocked or deficient. This helps to create an environment that is optimal for the body's function.

A toxic chemical, such as nicotine, alters the body's balance. Acupuncture restores balance to the extent that the chemical can be discarded without undue withdrawal symptoms.

So what might a quitting program be like with acupuncture? Some quitters require only one 45-minute session. During the session, the practitioner determines the course of treatment. He discusses diet and prescribes some herbs. Then a small, tacklike acupuncture needle is placed in the patient's ear. The patient is instructed to rub the tack if he has an urge to smoke. A follow-up session is scheduled for 48 hours after the initial treatment. And, for some quitters, that's it. The magic bullet.

Others require a more comprehensive course that might be ongoing and could include diet, herbs, more extensive acupuncture treatment, and some counseling. The time required for abstinence to be achieved varies from patient to patient.

The cost of these treatments varies from clinic to clinic, but typically the first session, including an intake interview, would cost from $100 to $150. Ongoing sessions would cost somewhat less.

When I inquired how people in Cucamonga would go about finding a legitimate acupuncturist, it was suggested that the searcher visit his local health food store; people there would likely know a local practitioner. Or let your fingers do the walking, and again, word of mouth is probably the best search tool.

In many states, acupuncturists are licensed by the state, and medical insurance will pay for the treatment. Be wary. Visit the acupuncturist's office. Ask for references.

Hypnosis

There are many uses and approaches to hypnotism. There are also many mistaken notions about the process.

It should be understood that hypnosis is always self-hypnosis. Another person only facilitates, teaches, guides, or directs the patient to a trance state.

Hypnosis has been described as a method of concentration. It is not sleep nor is it unconsciousness. It allows for a kind of parallel awareness, a double awareness that helps the mind become more receptive to its own thoughts.

Hypnosis is not a treatment, per se; rather, it is a facilitator of a treatment strategy. Nothing can be done with hypnosis that cannot be done without it. Hypnosis actually creates the atmosphere in which treatment strategies can be invoked. It need not be mysterious. It is measurable, teachable, and learnable.

A course of hypnosis as a tool for smoking cessation could take one to several one-hour sessions. During the initial session a history is taken. Then the patient is guided into a trance state, and suggestions are made by the therapist to the patient. For example,

"Smoking is a poison. Smoking is a poison to your body, not to yourself. Your body is a precious plant through which you live. You are your body's keeper. Respect your body. Because of your commitment to respect and care for your body, you have the power to smoke your last cigarette."

And so on. Notice the emphasis on positive action, the respect of the body.

Chapter Ten

The practitioner or therapist would likely give a suggestion, too, which instructs the quitter to do a simple exercise several times each day that would include self-suggestions about the cigarette as a poison and commitment to body health. The success of the quitting would determine the number of therapy sessions.

Hypnosis is practiced by M.D.s, Ph.D.s, and M.A.s. In most states they are licensed or accredited by the state. Your family physician should be able to assist you in finding a creditable hypnotherapist. Your local hospital might also be a resource. Look in the phone book. Be careful; there are some disreputable characters around. Visit the office. Ask for references, people who have stopped smoking with the assistance of the practitioner.

The cost would be the same as for any other therapist or counselor—from $100 to $200 per hour. I was unable to unearth any claims for successful cessation or abstinence rates.

I wouldn't be too hopeful about the people who run ads in the newspaper, who are passing through town and who say they can cure smoking with one $49.95 session at the such and such hotel. You can expect there to be a large crowd there. Some may quit for 20 minutes or so, but you can bet, this is not the magic bullet we seek.

Herbs, Homeopathy, and Other Remedies

People who come to my classes share remedies that they have purchased at the health food store and from other sources, such as herbologists and acupuncturists.

Joyce, for example, was using a homeopathic remedy called Natra-Bio, Smoking Relief. I found this on the Internet by going to *www.Google.com*, then keying in Natra-Bio. The cost was 48 tablets for $9.36, certainly less expensive than some of the other products I've discussed. Joyce found the product to be very helpful, and I believe it would be available at most health food stores. Joyce was also chewing on natural licorice sticks as a substitute for the cig, as she put it. She purchased these in the bulk grain section of the health food store. She also recommended sunflower seeds. I am hesitant to suggest nibbling constantly on seeds, because they can fatten you up just like anything else you eat a lot of.

Joyce and Jim both had a daily mug or two of yerba matte, a tea drink that enhances one's sense of well-being as well as the immune system. We have all heard in the past few years about the effectiveness of green tea as an immune system enhancer. I think yerba matte belongs to that category and apparently chases down those antioxidants and destroys them.

And Jim, along with daily trips to the acupuncturist, had a daily regimen of herb teas prescribed by his acupuncturist. He was convinced that these practices lessened the unpleasant feelings associated with nicotine withdrawal.

Karen, each morning, had a large veggie smoothie. She had another name for the concoction created by her children who owned a coffee store akin to Starbuck's. She availed herself of the largesse of this connection.

My friend Eddie brought to class and demonstrated a gismo called the JAI. The *Operations Manual and Use Instructions* said, "Restoring normalcy to the body's energy balance by utilizing the body's energy meridian points has been accomplished by many methods such as acupuncture, meditation and yoga. The JAI is the first non-invasive method of achieving this balance by using electrical currents at the same ultra-low levels at which the healthy body normally functions."

The JAI is a portable energy enhancer no larger than a small cell phone. A 9V battery powers the unit. The ultra-low current emitted by the unit is transferred to the body via wraps applied to selected areas of the body. The user feels either a slight tingle or nothing at all." Eddie used the wraps on his feet one night while he slept and said they made him feel clean and detoxed. The JAI can be rented by the month for $100 or can be purchased for $1,200. The address for more information about this device is JAI Energy Enhancer by EPRT Technologies, Inc. Pacific Palisades, CA 888-838-4008 *www.EPRTech.com.*

My mother-in-law picked up a flyer at the county fair that described "The Stop Smoking Pill." The product is supposed to help you "Stop Smoking Safely, Naturally, and Easily!" This pill was directed at the chemical loss of acetylcholine which, the brochure said, was an important component of withdrawal symptoms. "The active ingredient is shaped like the nicotine molecule and its nutrient action mimics nicotine but is nonaddictive." You can find out more about this product at *bcgr8house@qwest.net.* I have no idea about its efficacy, but I include this product to demonstrate that there are many things out there that make claims that they can help you.

On Google's Stop Smoking page, I came across *www.viableherbalsolutions.com.* I cannot vouch for this Web site but this is, again, to let you know that by going online or going to your health food store, you can find things that might assist you. There is lots of stuff out there for your use. Some of these products will help you restore health to your body and help you feel good about quitting cigarettes.

But, alas, none of this will do anything for you unless you have the determination, focus, and courage that it takes to become a nonsmoker. That's it, then. The End. It's time to quit cigarettes. I know you can do it. Remember, 44.8 million others have.

Appendix: Tobacco-Related Web Sites

American Cancer Society
www.cancer.org

American Lung Association
www.lungsusa.org

Americans for Nonsmokers' Rights
www.no-smoke.org

American Legacy Foundation
www.americanlegacy.org

National Cancer Institute
www.nci.nih.gov

Doctors Ought to Care
www.kickbutt.org

National Center for Tobacco Free Kids
www.tobaccofreekids.org

Nicotine Anonymous
www.nicotine-anonymous.org

Stop Teenage Addiction to Tobacco
www.stat.org

Dr. Linda Ferry et al.
www.findhelp.com

Heath Scout
www.healthscout.com

U.S. Health and Human Services Centers for Disease Control
www.cdc.gov/tobacco

Treatment Database and Educational Resource for Tobacco Dependence
www.treatobacco.net

World Health Organization
www.who.int

Action on Smoking and Health (ASH)
www.ash.org

Legacy Tobacco Documents Library
Http://legacy.library.ucsf.edu

Smokescreen Action Network (news service)
www.smokescreen.org

Joelle Publishing
www.joellepublishing.com
www.unfilteredtruth.com

Bibliography

"A Smoky Forecast." *U.C. Berkeley Wellness Letter* (July, 1998).

American Cancer Society. *Quitting Spitting: More Than Enough Reasons to Stop Using Spit Tobacco NOW!* American Cancer Society. 1996.

American Cancer Society. "Feminine Mistake." Film produced by Dave Bell Associates, Inc. Circa 1983.

"Articles." *Clinician's Research Digest: Briefings in Behavioral Science* 4, no. 8 (April 1986).

Becker, D. et al. "Smoking Behavior and Attitudes Toward Smoking Among Hospital Nurses." *American Journal of Public Health* 76, no. 12 (Dec. 1986): 1449.

Brokow, T. "Smoking in China," NBC Report, Nightly News (Mar. 1999).

Canadian Council on Tobacco. "Nicotine Replacement Therapies in Smoking Cessation: A Review of Evidence and Policy Issues." *www.globalink.org.* 2002.

Centers for Disease Control and Prevention. "Annual Smoking—Attributable Mortality, Years of Potential Life Lost, and Economic Costs – United States, 1995-1999. *MMWR* 51, no. 14 (April 12, 2002).

Centers for Disease Control and Prevention. *Best Practices for Comprehensive Tobacco Control Programs, 1999.* Atlanta, GA: U.S. Department of Health and Human Services, Centers for Disease Control and Prevention, 1999.

Centers for Disease Control and Prevention. "Cigarette Smoking Among Adults—United States, 1993." *MMWR* 43 (1994): 925-29.

Centers for Disease Control and Prevention. "Cigarette Smoking Among Adults—United States, 1999." *MMWR* 50, no. 40 (Oct. 12, 2000).

Centers for Disease Control and Prevention, Graph. "Percentage of adult ever smokers who are former smokers (prevalence of cessation), overall and by sex, race, Hispanic origin, age, and education, National Health Interview Surveys, selected years—United States, 1965-1995." Centers for Disease Control and Prevention (Nov. 2, 2000).

Centers for Disease Control and Prevention. "Use of FDA-Approved Pharmacologic Treatment for Tobacco Dependence – United States, 1984—1998." *MMWR* 49, no. 29 (July 28, 2000): 665-8.

Cherner, J.W. "Lorillard CEO dies of lung cancer." *www.SmokefreeAir.org.*

SmokeFree Educational Services, Inc. (Jan. 30, 2001).

Cummins, K. "Cigarette Makers Are Getting Away With Murder!" *Readers' Digest* (Sept. 1984): 72.

Decker, R. "Breaking Smoker's Ears and Noses" *Omni* 5 (Jan. 1983): 36.

Donkersloot, Mary & L. Ferry, M.D. *How To Quit Smoking and Not Gain Weight Cookbook.* Three Rivers Press, A Division of Random House, Inc. 1999.

Erdmann, J. "My Practice: Dr. Ferry Carves a Niche in Preventive Medicine." *ASAM News* (May-June 2001): 23.

Feldman, H.A. et al. "Impotence and Its Medical and Psychosocial Correlates: Results of the Massachusetts Male Aging Study." The Journal of Urology 151, no. 1 (Jan. 1994): 54-61.

"Few Stop Smoking on First Attempt: When Quitting, Try, Try Again." *Los Angeles Times*, Part 1 (January 16,1984): 12.

Fiore M.C., M.D. et al. *Treating Tobacco Use and Dependence, Clinical Practice Guideline.* Rockville, MD: U.S. Department of Health and Human Services Public Health Service. 2000.

Greenberg, R. et al. "Measuring the Exposure of Infants to Tobacco Smoke." *New England Journal of Medicine* (April 26, 1984): 1075-1078.

Lando, H.A. "Long-term Modification of Chronic Smoking Behavior: A Paradigmatic Approach." *Bulletin of the Society of Psychologists in Addictive Behaviors* 5, no. 1 (1986).

"Lozenges Help Smokers Quit." BBC Online (Oct. 29, 2001) *http://news.bbc.co.uk/hi/english/health/newsid_1622000/1622356.stm.*

Martin, M.J., S.C. Hunt. "Increased Incidence of Heart Attacks in Nonsmoking Women Married to Smokers." Paper presented at the 114th Annual Meeting of the American Public Health Association, Oct. 1, 1986.

Maugh, T. H. "Tobacco Smoke Harms Arteries, Study Finds." *L.A. Times,* (Jan. 14, 1998).

McCann, J. "Smoking in the Workplace Drains Profits, Productivity." *The Journal* (June 1984). Addiction Research Foundation, Canada.

Meier, B. "Cigarette Maker Manipulated Nicotine, Its Records Suggest." *New York Times* (Feb 12, 1998): A1.

Melville, N. "Tobacco Takes Toll On Bones: Experts say smoking increases fractures, slows healing." HealthScout News (Feb. 16, 2002). *Http://www1.excite.com/home/health_article/ 0,11720,504053,00.html.*

Mittlemark, M.B. et al. "Predicting Experimentation With Cigarettes: The Childhood Antecedents of Smoking Study (CASS)." *American Journal of Public Health* 77, no. 2 (Feb. 1987): 206.

Office on Smoking and Health, Fact Sheet. "The U.S. Economic Impact of Tobacco Use." Centers for Disease Control and Prevention (2001).

Office on Smoking and Health, Press Release. "State-Specific Adult Smoking Prevalence, Smokeless Tobacco Prevalence and State Tax-Paid Per Capita Sales of Cigarettes." Centers for Disease Control and Prevention, Office of Communication Media Relations (Nov. 6, 1998).

Office on Smoking and Health, Press Release. "Teens Still Exposed to Tobacco Ads Despite Advertising Restrictions." Centers for Disease Control and Prevention (Mar 7, 2002).

Phillips, R.S. et al. Eds. *Funk & Wagnall's New Encyclopedia* 24 (1983): 39-40.

Robicsek, F. *The Smoking Gods: Tobacco in Maya Art, History & Religion.* Norman, OK: University of Oklahoma Press, 1978.

Saunders, J. & H.M. Ross, M.D. *Hypoglycemia: The Disease Your Doctor Won't Treat.* New York: Pinnacle Books, 1980.

Schick Institute. *Questions and Answers About Habits. Smoking and Alcohol.* Los Angeles, CA: Schick Laboratories, 1980.

Schick's Smoke Signals. Los Angeles, CA: Schick Laboratories, July-Aug., 1985.

Seidell, J.C. et al. "The Relation Between Overweight and Subjective Health According to Age, Social Class, Slimming Behavior and

Smoking Habits in Dutch Adults." *American Journal of Public Health* 76, no. 12 (Dec.1986): 1410.

Severson, Herbert H., Ph.D. *Smokeless Tobacco, A Deadly Addiction.* Oregon Research Institute. Health Edco. 1997.

Severson, Herbert H., and Judith S. Gordon. *Enough Snuff: A Guide for Quitting Smokeless Tobacco.* Eugene, OR: Applied Behavior Science Press, 2000.

Skinner, B. F. *Science and Human Behavior.* New York: The Macmillan Company, 1953.

"Smoking and Impotence." California Department of Health Services Tobacco Control Section (June 1, 1998).

Society for Research on Nicotine and Tobacco et al. "Efficacy Database", 2002. *www.treatobacco.net.*

"Son's Death Prompts Mother to Sue Snuff Manufacturer." *The Press-Courier.* Washington Bureau, July 13, 1985.

"Study Adds Hearing Loss To Risks for Smokers," *Washington Post* (June 3, 1998): A10.

Task Force on Community Preventive Services. "Recommendations Regarding Interventions to Reduce Tobacco Use and Exposure to Environmental Tobacco Smoke." *American Journal of Preventive Medicine* 20, no. 2S (2001): 10-15.

U. S. Department of Health and Human Services. *Beat the Smokeless Habit: Game Plan for Success.* U.S. Department of Health and Human Services, National Institutes of Health. June 1993.

U.S. Department of Health and Human Services. "Chapter 4 – Management of Nicotine Addition." *Reducing Tobacco Use: A Report of the Surgeon General.* Atlanta: U.S. Department of Health and Human Services, Centers for Disease Control and Prevention, 2000.

U.S. Department of Health and Human Services. Public Health Service. *The 1986 Report of the Surgeon General on the Health Consequences of Smoking.* Rockville, MD: U.S. Department of Health and Human Services. Public Health Service.1986.

U.S. Department of Health & Human Services et al. *Spitting Into the Wind: The Facts About Dip and Chew.* U.S. Dept of Health and Human Services, et al. 1994.

U.S. Surgeon General's Advisory Committee on Smoking and Health. *Smoking and Health: Report of the Advisory Committee to the Surgeon General of the Public Health Service, U.S. Department of Health Education and Welfare.* Public Health Service, 1964.

Vlietstra, R. E. et al. "Effect of Cigarette Smoking on Survival of Patients with Angiographically Documented Coronary Artery Disease." Repost from CASS Registry. *Journal of American Medical Association* 225, no. 8 (Feb. 28, 1986).

Weil, Andrew, M.D. *Natural Health, Natural Medicine: A Comprehensive Manual for Wellness and Self-Care.* Boston: Houghton Mifflin Company, 1990.

---. "Superfood from the Sea." *Dr. Andrew Weil's Self Healing: Creating Natural Health for Your Body and Mind.* March 1998.

Index